COLOUR IN DECORATION

COLOUR IN DECORATION

Annie Sloan & Kate Gwynn

FRANCES LINCOLN

For our fathers

Frances Lincoln Limited
Apollo Works, 5 Charlton Kings Road
London NW5 2SB

Colour in Decoration
Copyright © Frances Lincoln Limited 1990
Text copyright © Annie Sloan and Kate Gwynn 1990

British Library Cataloguing in Publication Data

Colour in Decoration
Sloan, Annie
1. Interior Design
I. Title   II. Gwynn, Kate
747'.94

ISBN 0-7112-0604-X

Set in 11/12 pt and 12/13 pt Garamond 3 by Tradespools, Somerset
Printed in Hong Kong by Kwong Fat Ltd
First Frances Lincoln Edition: October 1990

1 3 5 7 9 8 6 4 2

CONTENTS

INTRODUCTION

Today's vast palette of colours is new and exciting. Any colour is at our fingertips, any combination of colours ours for the asking. This situation built up only gradually. Traditionally, wherever they lived, people used local colouring materials, so the redness or yellowness of their pigments depended very much on the colour of their local earth. Various plant dyestuffs and other pigments would be available locally, and every so often some traveller, new trade route or technological breakthrough brought new colours into play. Milestones such as these occurred when Far Eastern trade routes were opened up in the Middle Ages and new pigments such as indigo widened Europe's palette. When chemists developed synthetic aniline dyes in the mid nineteenth century, Western civilization endured a lurid phase of colours such as livid green and magenta. After World War I the quality of white was brightened and transformed with titanium dioxide, bringing an unprecedented pristine brilliance to twentieth-century paintwork.

As the palette available to them expanded, people began to evolve new ways of using colours. New worlds of colour opened up through travel, trade and conquest: those of the Aztec and Inca civilizations became known in Europe through the sixteenth-century Spanish conquistadors. The opening up of China to trade in the eighteenth century brought colours of a quite different quality to the attention of Western manufacturers and craftsmen. Individual travellers were struck by what they saw. During the eighteenth century, Europeans began to visit the many ancient sights of Rome, Greece and Egypt. Architects such as Robert Adam in Britain and Karl Friedrich Schinkel in Germany were among those who were inspired by what they found in Italy to use previously unheard-of combinations of brilliant colours – bright, clean pinks, blues, purples and greens.

Travel has continued to provide inspiration for colour schemes. However, 'imported' colour ideas will not necessarily translate successfully without judicious adaptation. The decoration of a Paris apartment may have been inspired by a brilliant riot of colours in a Mexican house, but the final impression will be tempered by the quality of light in northern Europe as well as by the style and period of the furniture and of the room.

The quality of light is significant. People in hotter climates tend to use pure colours which look vibrant and good in strong, bright light, while those in more temperate zones seem to mix their pigments to make more muted, softer colours. Very bright colours can look garish in places where the sun is weak. Conversely, the muted tweeds that look so right in Scotland look dirty and dull in the tropics.

Choice of colour is intensely personal. What is delicate and subtle to one person may well be insipid and drab to another; similarly, what one person calls 'cheerful' another will dismiss as garish. Furthermore, the same colour can be transformed when set against different backdrops – you may like it in one instance and loathe it in another.

Personal preference may be the starting point for choosing a colour; it is certainly the final criterion by which you should test a scheme you are contemplating. Associations provoked by different colours and colour combinations often have a profound effect on our mood and well-being. The advice of the experts and all the colour theory in the world will not have worked if you are not happy with the result.

Left Schinkel's choice of pale, bright pinks, greens and blues at Schloss Charlottenhof in East Germany was considered revolutionary in the late 1820s. This view gives us a good idea of the boldness of his palette.

Think of your favourite blue. It may be the deep, luminous glaze of a treasured ceramic, the slate-blue of a stormy seascape, the fragile clear colour of a bird's egg, the faraway misty texture of faded denim. Gazing at certain objects evokes a sense of pleasure. Your response is like that of an artist: you want to *use* that colour.

When you become aware of this sort of relationship with a colour, luxuriate in it. But also study what qualities so please you about it – its texture, depth and so on – and keep these at the back of your mind while you explore ways of using it.

What you are looking for may be a set of particular colours in combination – the pattern in a much-loved fabric, the colours of a favourite toy or book illustration, an object you have seen in a museum, the colours of the landscape of a happy holiday. In this case you have the core of a scheme ready-made.

Unpleasant associations, on the other hand, can turn us against a colour. Meditate on your own colour prejudices, because they sometimes cut across the entirely sensible theories of the 'experts'. And bear in mind that while 'gut reactions' play a significant role, it is also important – and exciting – to keep an open mind about the way colours behave in different combinations and in different contexts.

THE COLOUR WHEEL

This is a traditional device for representing the full range of colours in the spectrum and for demonstrating their relationship with one another. Its origin lies in the different wavelengths of light that produce the six colours that we see in a rainbow. In the wheel, the colours follow the same sequence as in the rainbow, but are brought round to meet in a circle. For convenience our wheel breaks them down into twelve distinct hues, although in reality the rainbow 'stripes' form a continuum, each colour gradually blending into its neighbour. The colour wheel also offers a useful demonstration of two other kinds of colour relationship:

Complementaries Complementary colours are those diametrically opposite each other on the colour wheel – red and green, blue and orange, crimson and lime green, and so on. They are the least like each other, offer most contrast and, when paired, produce visually stimulating effects – which we describe in 'Colour Behaviour' below.

Harmonies The hues that lie between two primary colours – say, crimson, violet and violet-blue – share a bias towards the secondary colour of that section (in this case violet) and are more harmonious than those that span a primary. The eye runs easily between them, without any abrupt transition. Even when they are seen out of sequence, a group of such related colours seems to belong together. A series of adjacent hues that spans a primary hue – lime green, yellow, yellow-orange – is naturally more discordant and needs more careful handling in a colour scheme.

Conspicuous by their absence from the colour wheel are black, white, brown, intermediate tones of grey and the neutral colours in which no distinct hue can be discerned. They are tremendously important in colour schemes but lie outside the scope of this wheel.

THE LANGUAGE OF COLOUR

In order to talk about the way colour works and to define what we mean, it is helpful to consider some of the vocabulary used in discussing the subject. Hue, intensity and tone are the terms used to describe aspects of the general make-up, or character, of a colour.

Left The colour wheel is a simple and comprehensive visual representation of how colours are perceived and the ways in which they are related to each other. Here you can see the basic principles of hue, complementaries and harmonies at work. A colour wheel can have as few as six colours – three primaries and three secondaries – or many more. This twelve-colour wheel includes tertiary colours.

Primary colours Blue, red and yellow are the three primary hues in their pure state, unmixed with any other colour.

Secondary colours Violet, orange and green represent a mixing of pairs of those colours: violet contains both red and blue, for example, and so on.

Tertiary colours These are colours made by mixing a primary and an adjacent secondary. Turquoise is a mixture of blue and green; lime green is a mixture of green and yellow; and crimson is a mixture of violet and red. The other tertiaries – orange-red, yellow-orange and violet-blue – have no established names.

Far left This illustration demonstrates the tonal variation of a colour as it moves from its purest state – represented in the middle of the tone band – into darker shades and lighter tints. A pure colour is one which is fully saturated and intense and has neither white nor black added to it. Some colours – blue, for example – have a wide tonal range while others, such as yellow or orange, are more limited in scope. Strictly speaking, there are no such colours as 'dark orange' or 'dark yellow' – orange becomes brown as it gets darker while yellow turns to a rather indeterminate greeny brown, as is apparent here. In decoration, colour harmony can be achieved either by using colours together which share the same tonality or by combining different tones of the same colour.

There are, of course, many factors that affect the nature of a colour: the medium with which a colour is combined is, for example, important. In paint, the pigment – or dry, powdered colouring material – is suspended in an oil- or water-based medium and then applied to a surface. Colours in a medium that dries flat look different from the same colours mixed in a medium that dries to a sheen. Similarly, the texture of a surface, whether rough or smooth, will significantly affect the colour with which it is painted or, in the case of textiles, impregnated.

Hue is the word used to designate the quality of a colour that gives it its position on the colour wheel, its particular degree of, for example, redness, blueness or greenness.

Intensity, or saturation, refers to purity, brightness and denseness. When a colour is of maximum intensity or saturation, it is strong, bright and clean. The opposite of an intense colour is one that is dulled, 'knocked back', muted or 'dirty'.

Tone is the word used to define the darkness or lightness of a colour: shades (dark tones) of blue are darker than the hue – moving towards black – and tints (light tones) are closer to white. The hues of the colour wheel have intrinsic tonal values, too. Yellow is the

Reds and blues can work together in different ways. **Right** The bright magenta and purple-blue are not only of similar intensity but are also close to each other on the colour wheel and thus appear harmonious. The white wall and ceiling offset their brightness. **Far right** Pale tints of the same colours decorate this verandah. Although also harmonious in hue and tone, they are dissimilar in texture and create a very different atmosphere. The powdery blue and pink have been muted and lightened to the same degree so that they seem almost to blend together. White is not needed.

lightest in tone, violet the darkest. Green and red have a similar tonal value: they would appear to be much the same shade of grey, providing almost no tonal contrast, in a black-and-white photograph of the colour wheel.

COLOUR BEHAVIOUR

Various effects are produced when different colours are put together. One well-known optical 'trick' is achieved by staring at a red dot for some time and then looking away at a plain white piece of paper. You will find that a green dot appears. This illusory green dot is called the after-image, and it is always the complementary of the colour you have stared at. In this case, it is what the eye needs as a respite from the intense red.

Decorators exploit this phenomenon when a touch of orange, say, is introduced to relieve the uniformity of an all-blue scheme: the orange, blue's complementary, provides what the eye is looking for. In this sort of example you will often find that the hues employed are not pure: 'muted' versions of orange, such as burnt orange or apricot, are effective in counterbalancing the blues.

Problems arise when complementary colours are given equal weight in a decorative scheme and are both used at full intensity. The eye finds it impossible to focus on both colours at the same time, and the attempt sets up an uncomfortable flickering sensation. If one, or both, of the colours is muted in some way, or if one colour is allowed to predominate, the result can be lively without being uncomfortable.

Quirks of perception are also behind other qualities of colour – those described as advancing and receding. Science can explain why distant hills always look blue, why red flowers appear much closer than the green foliage that surrounds them, and why yellow possesses optimum visibility in a city context – a fact that made it the obvious choice for American taxicabs. These attributes are recognized in decorating home truths such as red walls 'advance' and make a room seem smaller, blue walls 'recede' and give a room a feeling of spaciousness, and bright yellow is attention-seeking, so, as a general rule, a little can go a long way.

Advancing and receding colours are paralleled by those termed warm and cold. Colours based on the yellow-orange-red part of the spectrum seem warm and immediate; the greater their intensity, the more they seem to project forward, so comparatively small amounts do seem to go a long way, and larger quantities make a 'hot' scheme. Violet-blues, blues, green-blues and black appear to recede and so create a feeling of space. The blues and violets are generally thought of as 'cool' colours. Beware of assumptions about warm and cool schemes and colours, however. Paint colours are subtly muted and modified by mixtures of pigments, and icy pinks and crimsons can be distinctly cool. Similarly a green-blue to which a touch of yellow has been added can appear vibrant and warm – a far cry from the coolness often associated with blue.

Below Changing the wall colour behind these shelves from green to purple transforms the overall effect. Both are, however, examples of harmonious colour schemes that cross a primary hue. The combination of greens, yellows and oranges in the first is bright and lively. The purple background in the second, although more sombre, is subtly enhanced by blues and yellow-greens.

The quality of a colour depends very much on the quality of the light illuminating it. Daylight affects colour by moulding the objects on which it falls, creating highlights and casting shadows. Imagine a room in which all the surfaces and objects are painted in the same colour. Even this unmitigatedly monochromatic scheme would be brought to life by light. The wall opposite the window would look several shades lighter than the window wall itself. Some areas would be in deep shadow, shiny surfaces would reflect a whitish gleam, and so on. Artificial lighting would create a variety of different effects and for this reason it is sensible to colour-match fabrics, wallpaper and paint in good daylight and then compare them under artificial light. The yellowish tone of light from standard incandescent bulbs will 'warm' any surface on which it falls; fluorescent lights will have a harsh, bluer cast. Some colours change dramatically even under incandescent light. Yellows, especially pale ones, tend to 'disappear', terracottas turn orange, mid greens turn yellow-green and purples become brown. While colour-corrected bulbs are available, they are expensive and mostly used in special situations, such as artists' studios.

Above At a glance, it is hard to believe that these photographs are of the same room, simply shown from different ends – one in natural, the other in artificial light. In natural light, the lit areas of the wall and table are brighter, the rest, in shadow, are seen here almost in outline. In artificial light, there are few shadows and the variety of colours, tones and textures is all-apparent.

Above and right Monochromatic schemes can be enlivened by the use of contrasting textures and decorative detailing, as demonstrated in these two interiors. The colour-washed wall of a New York hallway (above) provides a cool setting for the warmth of the carved gilded table and mirror. The ochre in the marbling and the umber of the clay pots extend the range of neutrals. A similar combination of colours and materials has been put to use in the London drawing room (right). Again, a variety of gentle neutral colours is combined with natural textures and surfaces to create a soothing atmosphere. The gilding and the rich hues of the wooden floor add depth and warmth to the room.

COLOUR SCHEMES

Most schemes fall into one of the following broad categories. In the first three you are aware of links, similarities and affinities between the ingredients; in the others, contrasts and differences are exploited, so that objects stand out from one another rather than blending and merging together.

Monochromatic schemes involve choosing one hue and using it throughout a room, varying its tone and intensity. There need to be deep-coloured areas, mid tones and highlights. This may sound straightforward enough, but the variation that can be achieved within a monochromatic scheme is enormous, at a glance so large a variation of colour that you might not recognize it immediately as monochromatic, although this accounts for why it 'works' so well. You get more interesting effects with yellows, reds and oranges than with the deeper toned blues, violets and greens. A cool yellow hue, for instance, when softened and muted turns greyish green, and when deepened in tone appears olive green – its yellowness is completely hidden. A green-blue hue, on the other hand, is recognizable as such in all its tints, shades and muted versions.

Monochromatic schemes can also be based on the neutral colours, such as bleached white, sand, or beige; these are often teamed with natural or organic textures like wood, stone, shell, hessian or coir that have a colour affinity.

Besides creating subtle variations of tone and intensity to make a monochromatic scheme interesting, you can relieve the single-colour effect by providing strong textural contrasts with other materials: metal, such as chrome, brass, or stainless steel; glass or mirror; polished wood, stone or marble. These materials may have an intrinsic colour,

like the 'yellow' of brass, but the gleam of the surface gives it a far more abstract quality – almost like that of pure light.

Finally, it is important to recognize that many successful schemes that appear to be monochromatic are in fact understated versions of one of the 'contrast' principles, in which one colour predominates overwhelmingly but is brought to life by subtle touches of other appropriate colours.

Harmonies of hue Hues that blend into one another on the spectrum wheel will also blend well in a decorative scheme. They do not have to be of the same tone or intensity, or be used in the same proportions.

Harmonies of tone and intensity An even broader range of hues can be safely brought into play if the hues are of a similar tonal value or intensity. Decorative schemes based on this principle can give a pleasing sense of colour affinity without following a strict colour rule. Victorian polychrome designs are often good illustrations of this sort of scheme; since the hues are also muted to the same degree, they have the same 'flavour'. This principle is also exploited in many modern multicoloured wallpaper and fabric designs.

Above left The colour gradation of these studio walls at Charleston, West Sussex, has been very precisely created to achieve a subtle harmony of hue. Set between cool greys and blue-greens, the comparative warmth of the soft, muted bluish red is accentuated.

Above right Blue, green and grey work well together in this simply decorated room because they share a harmony of hue and tone – each is a gently muted but clean colour. The natural colour of the ceiling and the background of the spattered walls provides a light but muted effect, giving the room a restful atmosphere.

Below left This modern hallway is an example of a primary colour scheme used with style and confidence. When placed together in the same degrees of intensity, the three primary colours tend sometimes to cancel each other out. But it is a colour combination that works particularly well when, as here, one of the three colours has been softened slightly – the yellow and red are of the same intensity while the blue is subtly muted. In this scheme, the 'yellow' wall colour is an effect produced from the passage of light through the yellow-painted glass of the vertical windows on to what is, in fact (and what would indeed appear at night to be), a white wall.

Below right The bold, broad lines of blue and yellow in this study show how colours of contrasting tone can work together to excellent effect. The boldness of the wallpaper is matched by the black-and-white stripes of the upholstered chair.

Contrasts of tone Among the most striking schemes based on contrasts of tone are those that pair black and white, the extremes of the dark-to-light scale. Black with yellow – the lightest hue – and white with blue or violet – the darkest hue – make almost as strong a contrast as black and white.

Primary schemes In these only primary colours are used. The colours have a striking resonance because they are equally strong and intense and, as a result, can be quite hard on the eye. Modernist designers used primary colours effectively by setting them against white.

Complementary schemes The simplest of these are those based on pairs of opposites as shown on the colour wheel. Generally a larger area of the cooler, receding colour is 'balanced' by smaller quantities of the more advancing complementary, and either or both colours are modified in tone and intensity. This balance is achieved when, for instance, one colour is used to cover a sofa and the other is used for piping the cushions.

Split-complementary schemes Here, in strict definition, three colours from the colour wheel are used. One colour is matched not with its complementary, but with the pair of colours on either side of it. But because the colour wheel can include as few as six colours or many more, one can also create a split complementary from a range of colours close to the exact complementary. Green would be teamed not with red but with violet and orange. Here the intensity of the colours could certainly be varied: the green might be kept brilliant, while the orange is lightened with some white and the violet deepened and muted to become a blue-brown.

Your starting point for making choices may be an exciting colour – something that sets the key of the whole scheme. It could be a preference – a colour you love and feel you must use and, if so, it may very well already be a theme in some of your possessions (a collection of glass or china or a rug, painting, chair). An object – ethnic rug, lacquer tray, ceramic plate – may contain a combination of colours that you can take and expand as a ready-made theme. Or you can create a colour scheme around fabrics, cushions, pictures and other accessories.

Sometimes a room contains a strong colour that you have to work around: a tiled fireplace-surround, a carpet, sofa or bathroom suite that you are not free to replace. To make a virtue of such necessities, a practical working knowledge of colour is essential; with the right choice of neighbouring colours, what may appear to be a singularly uninspiring

Above Red and green are complementaries used simply and boldly in this early-American bedroom. They are juxtaposed elegantly with white in patterned quilts, and their colours are picked up subtly and effectively in the green woodwork and in the red curtain rings.

Above This cosy, intimate study shows its colours best at night, when the warmth and strength of the reds, yellows and browns are brought out by electric light. A light-coloured, elegantly checked armchair provides a subtle contrast to the darker colours of the bookshelf.

starting point for an interior scheme can be completely transformed.

If your home belongs to a particular style or period, you could consider whether the original decorating scheme provides inspiration. If you have moulded cornices and ceiling plasterwork, or striking woodwork, you might take a cue from the palette of the period. It is not necessary to take historical authenticity too literally, but refer to the tones used and perhaps blend them with colours that make them work today. For a 1930s apartment, you might choose light, muted colours or neutrals, contrasted with chrome or lacquered surfaces. If you decide to create your own scheme, at least keep it in tune with the surroundings: sharp, synthetic colours, for example, can look out of place in an ochre-coloured stone cottage in the countryside.

The function of a room must also be taken into account when devising a colour scheme. As a general rule, rooms that are not frequently used can take stronger colours. Similarly, rooms that are usually only used at night may need deeper, stronger colours in order to off-set the yellowing effect of incandescent light bulbs. Aspect, too, is an important factor. In a room with small windows, it may be possible to create more light by using pale, reflective colours.

In this book we hope to stimulate your interest in colours and how they work together. The main part of the book, the 'Portraits', is divided into broad colour sections. We chose the pictures in each to indicate the range within any one colour and to inspire you to use a mixture of colours that may be new to you. We have tried to show how colours look together and how the combination can create a sumptuous or simple interior.

The section on palettes discusses how some groups of colours have evolved in different parts of the world for various climatic, cultural, historical and geographic reasons. The relationship between the colours in each group, their intensity and the different tonal values they have, influence the creation of a particular atmosphere. These colours can be used as a base for your own room, or they may be used to spark off other ideas.

Good colour mixing is the key to successful interiors and the basic rules are really quite simple. At the end of the book we provide a section to show how colours can be mixed. This is most important: many people have attempted to mix one colour only to end up with a large amount of another, unwanted one. You can make your own paint colours using the recipes we have provided, or study the colour mixing pages to gain the knowledge you need to ask for the colours you want.

In the end, there can be no set formulas for colour mixing and colour-use, but we hope the guidelines we provide will help you make your decorating less of a hit-and-miss affair and the creative process lots of fun.

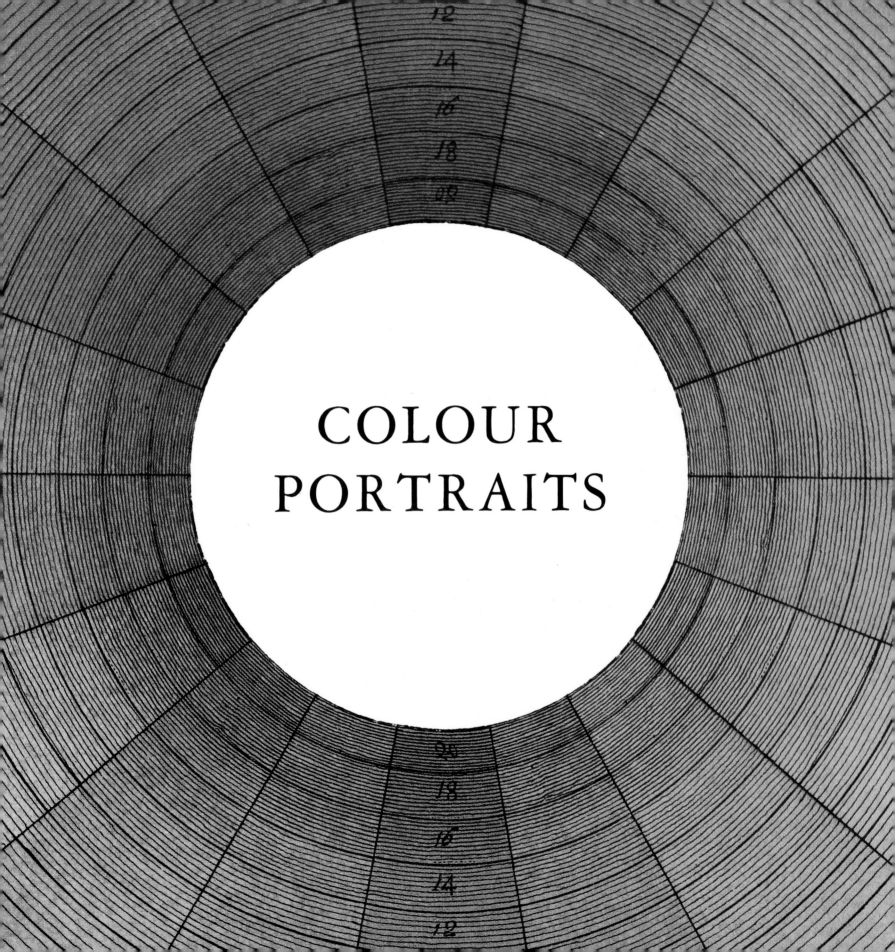

COLOUR
PORTRAITS

YELLOW

COOL YELLOW

The clear, strong and luminous cool yellows range from the gleam of winter jasmine to the vivid brilliance of the mimosa flower.

The colour does not have a long decorating history since it was not possible to mix a vivid cool yellow from yellow ochre, even when an organic yellow was added. It was not until the 1820s, when chrome yellow was manufactured cheaply enough for it to be generally available, that a clear, bright and reliable yellow was included in the house painter's palette.

Clear lemon yellow was popular in the Empire period when it was contrasted with amethyst and at the end of the nineteenth century it was often combined with green. It continued in vogue through the 1920s and 1930s and was also a popular colour in the 1950s, particularly for fabrics, when it was teamed with white, black and grey.

These yellows find their complement in reddish mauves – it is generally more successful to use a hint of the complementary and to let the yellow predominate. Pale and blue-greys combine particularly well with cool yellow while white can always be used to

Left Monet's house at Giverny has recently been restored and repainted following the original colour scheme. The yellow dining room – along with the blue kitchen – is the centrepiece of the house. It is painted in two tones of cool yellow, offset by bright blues in fabric and china.

Right The spacious drawing room of Sir John Soane's house at Lincoln's Inn Fields in London has been restored to its 1830s brilliance with yellow paintwork, curtains and upholstery. It is one of the first rooms that we know of where fabric and paint have been consciously co-ordinated. The original wall colour was mixed using patent yellow which was then varnished to lend it stability. To re-create the colour, chrome yellow was mixed with white oil paint and coated with a clear eggshell (mid-sheen) varnish. The ceiling was painted a dull white, which the reflection of the yellow walls turns almost creamy. The fine red borders of the silk curtains, the red braid on the sofa and the touches of black articulate the elegant lines of the curtains and furniture. The red is a warm earth red, not a crimson. Despite the strength of the colours, the room has a light, meditative feel.

offset it. This colour also looks effective when placed with the range of warmer blues.

Alternatively, you can team cool yellow with those colours that lie on either side of it in the spectrum – the greens and warmer yellows and reds. Many successful fabrics are based on this combination.

In their most saturated form, cool yellows can seem sharp, almost metallic, and they are well suited to the clear lines of a modern interior. They can work well with black plastic, chrome and shiny surfaces and with other luminous colours.

The cool yellows can be mixed using chrome lemon or cadmium lemon.

Left A corner of the garden room at Charleston in West Sussex, once the home of Vanessa Bell and Duncan Grant. The curtains and pelmet are of 'Grapes' fabric, 1931, designed by Duncan Grant for Alan Walton Ltd and recently made available again from Laura Ashley. The walls of the room were left undecorated until 1945 and the present stencilled pattern was probably designed by Vanessa Bell; she and Duncan Grant painted it. The colours are sympathetic to each other. The lemon-peel yellow of the curtains and shutters contrasts tonally with the grey colours of the walls but they share a common cool yellowness. The soft brown of the painted cupboard, the leaves and the violin, tones well with the other colours while adding a note of warmth to the room.

Right The wall colour and the patterned carpet of this elegant bedroom share the same, underlying, cool yellow hue. The soft white of the tablecloth and bedlinen freshens and enlivens the yellow while the blue-grey of the 'neo-classical' pictures, the fabric bow and the broad-striped upholstery add a cool note of contrast. Small touches of red in the cushion and lampshades and a confident use of black and gold complete the picture.
Designer: Mark Hampton

Right A Swedish textile designer here mixes colours and periods in a confident and eclectic way. An elegant Gustavian sofa rubs shoulders with 1940s ceramics, a teak table and a floor lamp from the 1950s. The yellow paintwork provides a light toned backdrop for the stronger colours – black, vermilion, primary blue, turquoise and lime green. There are no muted or pastel shades.
Designer: Ingel Hakansson-Lamm

Above The kitchen-dining room of a converted warehouse in Melbourne, Australia, combines yellow and grey to good effect. The walls and ceilings are painted in cream while the floor is covered with soft grey vinyl. The bright lemon and dark grey laminates introduce vibrant touches of colour to the overall scheme.

Right This artist's studio and family home is a converted Victorian dancing school. The walls are painted a cool yellow, against which furniture and paintings are clearly defined. The brilliant white of the painted floor and ceiling matches the tone of the yellow and maximizes the effect of light and brightness in the room.

WARM YELLOW

Warm yellow recalls the colours of buttercups, sunflowers and, in its darkest shades, amber. It is a gentle, golden hue – a yellow with a hint of red.

Whereas the pure bright yellows derive from the deep chromes and the cadmiums, the darker shades are made from the more soothing yellow ochres which produce a warm golden colour.

This yellow is a traditional decorating colour that featured in the earliest house painter's palette. Its use in the Classical period ensured its popularity in neo-classical interiors of the late eighteenth century.

The vividness of the more luminous of the warm yellows makes them a good choice for sophisticated interiors

Left This London drawing room was once the home of Nancy Lancaster, owner of Colefax and Fowler, the interior design company. It demonstrates her imaginative use of colour and a sense of style characteristic of her partner, John Fowler. The emphasis was on yellow rather than cream, which in the 1950s when the room was decorated was considered a breakthrough. The walls were painted in a mid-yellow semi-gloss paint which gives the room a feeling of spaciousness and light that epitomizes English style. It always looks sunny, even on a dark day. The ceiling was painted in three subtle tones of beige and the silk curtains were made up in two shades of golden yellow. Touches of lemon yellow, marigold, red and turquoise were added by the upholstery. The yellow background of the Ukrainian rug sets the theme.

Right The inspiration for this colour scheme was drawn from Sir John Soane's drawing room. Deep cadmium yellow in an oil glaze was dragged over white eggshell (an oil base) to create a warm, luminous look. The ceiling and dado were painted in off-white flat oil 'dirtied' with raw umber. The room's thin paper borders – just visible here behind the chair and above the bookcase – painted an earth red, pull the design together and pick up the reds and pinks used in the upholstery. *Designers: John and Gabrielle Sutcliffe*

because these shades tend to be light-enhancing and benefit from large rooms and open spaces.

Warm yellow can make a good wall colour that is offset well by white ceilings and skirtings. It combines effectively with ornaments, pictures, patterned fabrics and with rich and strong colours: darker reds, blues, greens and blacks. Even turquoise can look good with it, although the contrast with its complementary, bluish purple, is sometimes too harsh to be successful. Attractive, softer results can come from teaming warm yellow with more neutral or cooler colours such as lead grey, light brown, celadon green, lavender or a subtle grey-blue. When used in a glaze or distressed finish or with dark colours or rich woods, warm yellow can look bright, clear and lustrous.

When more muted or deeper in tone, this yellow is well suited to small rooms to which it can add depth.

Above All the colours in this room are warm – from the distressed egg-yolk walls to the madder-red *toile de Jouy* fabric. A soothing white has been used to link these hot colours. The wall effect has been achieved using a thinned down butterscotch emulsion (water-based paint) over a coat of flat, pale dusty yellow emulsion. *Decorator: Robin Knapp*

Right Warm yellow is used as the main colour in this artist's drawing room where a slightly shiny fabric in the same colour as the walls has been chosen for the elegant Empire-style sofa. The dark green curtains and the red in the carpet add contrast.

Far right These walls are painted a brilliant deep yellow, made up of yellow ochre and raw umber, partly rolled, partly sponged and partly rubbed on over a base of white emulsion. The colour conveys an atmosphere of cosiness, despite the size of the room. The faded red and gilt chairs and the touches of black add a richness which is offset by the simple, cotton canvas curtains. *Decorator: Keith Day*

Below This large sunny kitchen in a converted eighteenth-century rectory glows with warmth. Light streaming in from the garden picks up the warm earth tones of the ceramic floor tiles and the rich hues of the solid ash furniture. The walls have been washed with a yellow ochre glaze above the olive green dado. Stencilled triglyphs and terracotta medallions echo the neo-classical theme of the room. *Decorator: Johnny Grey for Smallbone*

Left This bedroom was painted for his maid by the Swedish artist, Carl Larsson. The warm yellow walls are bordered by a broad, somewhat naively painted, blue-green frieze and a thin earthy orange ceiling fillet. These strong colours are softened by the white ceiling, the white bed-canopy and the pale grey paint of the bed. The rag rug mixes stripes of green, earthy orange and dark blue.

Above The colours and textures of Africa inspired the decoration of this striking room. The soft yellow walls, coconut floor matting and natural wooden furniture all represent the warm, neutral colours often associated with the African landscape. They contrast well with the brighter colours and patterns and the textures of the woven fabrics. Because there are no primary, or artificial colours here, the contrasts are lively but not loud or overwhelming.

PALE YELLOW

This colour can be buttery or a cool and crisp primrose yellow. Pale yellows – somewhat lighter versions of the colours used in English Empire and Regency houses – were popular in American Colonial and Federal interiors of the late eighteenth and early nineteenth centuries.

The slightly greenish yellow of primrose works well with hues and shades of its complementary, reddish purple – this combination will give life and warmth to interior schemes. Used with cool blues, greys and whites, pale yellow appears soft and warm. Warmer hues – which can be mixed from yellow ochre – look their clearest when combined with browns and blacks. Pale yellows are usually made from cadmium or chrome yellows to which some white has been added.

Above This simple and unpretentious scheme relies on colour rather than on the lavishness of decorative details. The fresh yellows bring light to a dark city basement and the bright colours of the rag rug, which include violet – yellow's true complementary – add zest to the picture. The cushions and the spray of flowers introduce additional touches of violet.

Right The owner of this farmhouse mixed a lilac Moroccan powder paint with milk and applied it over a white base on the walls of her sitting room. The result is a soft, almost chalky colour, a gentle and pleasing complement to the soft yellow of the fireside cupboard. *Artist: Amanda Feilding*

Far right A generally harmonious colour scheme – composed of pale tints of yellow, gold and terracotta – is enriched by touches of warm red and brown. The bunch of delphiniums and the blue-and-white china add a few notes of colour contrast to the decoration of this house in the Hudson Valley. *Designer/decorator: David Easton*

DULL YELLOW

Below In the hallway of this house in Gran Canaria, the plaster walls have been painted to look like crumbling blocks of stone by stippling a range of ochres, umbers and whites in different combinations. The deep olive eggshell (mid-sheen, oil-based) paint of the doorway harmonizes with the honey tones of the walls. The *trompe l'oeil* effect is continued in the skirting board, painted grey to simulate stone. *Owner/designer: Christophe Gollut. Artist: André Dubreuil*

Undemanding and restful to the eye, this range of yellows is produced from the natural pigments, ochre and raw sienna, that occur in clays and sands in many parts of the world. They have always been cheap and easy to obtain and have a long history in both interior and exterior house painting and decoration. Ochres were the yellows of the house painter's traditional palette – as popular in Africa and Scandinavia as in Italy and Provence,

as common on a mud hut as on a Venetian palace. They lend mellow warmth to any interior.

If dull yellow is used with cool greys and blues its yellowness is accentuated whereas alongside other warm, earthy colours it appears more neutral.

Mix dulled yellow from yellow ochre and/or raw sienna – a brownish yellow – and white; add raw umber to dull or mute the colour.

Above Ancient Assyria provided the inspiration for the treatment of this room, but the colours used would look wonderful in any setting. Yellow ochre, raw sienna and raw umber pigments were used to colour white acrylic gesso, which was then applied in six layers, on top of existing plaster, each layer being sanded down in between – as in the preparation of an Italian panel painting on gesso. Finally, the walls were sealed with a clear lacquer to retain their subtle textures and colouring. The overall design was drawn together by the darker raw umber of the frieze which adds definition to the room.
Artist: Veronica Hudson

Left In the scullery of Christophe Gollut's house in Gran Canaria, the turquoise blue of the corner cupboard is a sharp contrast to the dull mustard yellow of the rough plaster walls.

ORANGE

The yellow-orange and orange colours represented here range from pale apricot, peach and melon tints through to the richer, warmer tones of the fruit from which the colour's name is derived.

Pale yellow-orange and deep orange were popular in the design schemes and fabrics of the Art Nouveau and Art Deco movements and in 1960s interiors.

Because of their warmth, oranges need cool colours to act as a contrast and counterbalance. Most cool greens and blues work well with them. Blue is the true complementary.

Yellow-orange may be mixed from intense colours such as cadmium yellow and a little cadmium red but these tend to produce a hot, rather harsh effect, which, when white is added, can give a bland and over-sweet pale apricot. The trick is to make these colours from a slightly earthier base such as burnt sienna or light red. Add a touch of cadmium yellow or yellow ochre to this to give warm oranges. The addition of white softens the colour and makes a range of melon to apricot hues, which are complex and interesting.

Above Let nature provide inspiration. The orange, yellow ochre and lime green of this dried flower arrangement could provide a starting point for a successful and harmonious scheme.

Left A single colour can be used throughout a room to create a soothing and harmonious atmosphere. Here the pale, yellow-orange walls provide the lightest tone and a background for the slightly browner sofa and the rich silk curtains while offering a dramatic contrast with the large, dark painting. The fine detailing on the cushions and sofa frame adds variety of texture, tone and pattern.

Far left The stippled, melon-coloured, wallpaper gives warmth to the spacious hallway of this country house. The colour reflects light well and prevents any sense of gloominess in an area which can be quite dark during the day. The contrasting chocolate brown of the paper border adds definition. The elegant white banisters stand out boldly against the varying grey hues of the polished eighteenth-century flagstones.
Designer: David Hicks

Above Introduce splashes of orange into decorating schemes by way of eyecatching fabrics such as these.

Right A bold use of deep orange-yellow in the entrance hall of this house, which once belonged to Carl Larsson, creates a space that is both warm and inviting. The richness of the orange is counterbalanced by a cool green; the white of the doorframe and corner shelf provides a crisp contrast to these two colours, drawing the scheme together and preventing it from being overpowering.

Far right Inspired by the print rooms of the eighteenth century, black-and-white printed paper borders, swags and ribbons have been laboriously cut out and pasted down to frame a collection of pen and ink drawings. Straying somewhat from tradition, a warm orange has been used as the background colour, turning a small dark lobby into a little jewel box. The protective coat of varnish on the walls has a slight tinge of yellow. *Designer: Nicola Wingate-Saul*

RED

BROWN-RED

Rich brown-reds are natural, comforting colours that are often introduced into interior schemes unobtrusively in the form of polished woods, dark baked tiles or earthenware pots rather than as overall wall or fabric colours. They are frequently referred to as terracotta, meaning literally 'baked earth'.

These colours go well with all related shades of warm red, with the other earth pigments, yellow ochre and umbers, and with blues and greens. Used in varying tones, they are particularly effective when placed with a comparable range of blues, from soft to very sharp, which can make a striking contrast. The Egyptians mixed these colours with an unerring eye and their frescoes are one of the best sources of design inspiration. The colour's widespread use during the Classical period made it fashionable with neo-classical architects and designers. The Victorians combined brown-red floor tiles with cream, black and mid blue, a colour scheme sometimes echoed on walls, paintwork and fabrics.

Left A simple cupboard painted in a strong brown-red provides an ideal background for a display of blue-and-white Delft china and an arrangement of cottage-garden flowers including phlox, larkspur and cornflowers.

Above The warm, earthy orange-reds, reddish browns and cool blues of the ancient Egyptian palette can provide inspiration for decorating schemes. Traditionally, the Egyptians used black charcoal to depict hair, white lime for clothes, yellow and red ochre for the bodies of humans and animals; minerals such as malachite and azurite produced green and blue pigments. The balance and harmony which can be achieved using these colour combinations is shown in

this fresco dating from the fifteenth century BC, from the tomb of Nebamun near Thebes.

Right A large stove, built from brick and covered with glazed tiles, gives a strong focus to the drawing room of an eighteenth-century Finnish manor house furnished in Biedermeier style. The rich red-brown colour is picked up by similar tones in the two chairs and complemented by the intense blue of the distemper. Pale wooden floorboards and a white ceiling are an ideal neutral context for the stronger colours, while a painted paper frieze adds definition to the room. The scenic French wallpaper dates from 1830 and shows the bustling harbour at Marseilles.

ORANGE-RED

The orange-reds are soothing, earthy colours, strong and bright without being overpowering. They lack the aggressiveness of red or the exuberance of orange but convey the subdued warmth of the range of coral tones.

The colour became very popular at the beginning of the nineteenth century, as a result of the discovery of the wall paintings at Pompeii. Used frequently in matt tones, it was often incorporated as a wall colour in drawing rooms.

Orange-reds derive originally from earth reds and burnt yellow ochres, both of which are iron oxides occurring naturally throughout the world. They have always been inexpensive, extremely stable pigments.

Brown-red harmonizes well with this shade of red, as does a warm pale red and black. If the red is more orange, it finds its complement in turquoise blue, if more scarlet, in green.

Above Writing in 1827, John Britton observed that Sir John Soane's library and dining room had been painted 'a deep red colour in imitation of the walls of Herculaneum and Pompeii'.

The room's details have a dull bronzed finish – an effect achieved by flicking bronze powder on to a green lacquer base. This technique, often employed by Soane and his contemporaries, was also thought to have been used in ancient Rome.

Right The former studio of the artist Augustus John has acquired an exoticism from its present Middle Eastern owners. The rich patterning of deep oranges, terracottas and reds is enhanced by touches of azure and turquoise. *Designer: Hamoush Bowler*

Above In this nineteenth-century design for the ceiling of a French town house, orange-red is shown in combination with green and neutral colours.

Right The colours of Carl Larsson's dining room are similar – if slightly more yellow – to those used by Sir John Soane some 70 years earlier, although the green has been left plain, not bronzed. Warm orange-red was considered a good colour for dining rooms and green is its natural complementary. The single chair has been painted in a deeper shade of the orange-red, a dark brown-red – a colour which is also picked up in the woven fabrics. When this room was painted in the 1890s, the colours and colour combinations used were the subject of much controversy.

Left The interplay of orange-red and greeny blue can work to powerful effect in interior decoration, as evident in this view from the painted wooden archway of a house in Marrakesh, Morocco. The walls are painted pale orange-pink, a colour that is perfectly balanced by the cool green-blue tones of the door, the arches and the cupboard. A floor colour of cool pink completes the scheme.

Right In the library at Charleston, once the home of Vanessa Bell and Duncan Grant in West Sussex, a range of light coral, orange-red and rich reddish brown colours creates an inviting and harmonious atmosphere. The distinctive pale orange-pink of the wooden window panels – painted by Duncan Grant – is picked up by similar tones in the kilims, the spines of the books, and the decorated bookcase. These colours are complemented by the green woodwork of the late-eighteenth-century chairs and by touches of blue, green and greeny blue elsewhere in the room. The pale pink chair fabric and the white ceiling and skirting board introduce cool contrast, freshness and light.

PALE WARM PINK

Pale warm pinks are the colour of fresh wall plaster and the inside of conch shells, varying to include orange and pale brown shades. They are soft, natural colours, well suited to vernacular buildings, relaxing and easy to live with. Because of their paleness, they are often best used to cover large surfaces – such as walls – as, in small quantities, they are easily overwhelmed by other colours.

The complementaries of the warm pinks are the blue-greens, but they harmonize with most other pale earthy colours and all shades of warm red. To make a more lively composition, add a splash of crimson or orange.

Above These walls have been plastered in a traditional, soft pink colour that works well with the earthy greens. To accentuate colour and texture, the final plaster skim was applied using a wooden rather than a metal float. *Designer: Annie Sloan*

Left This view of the swimming pool area of an eighteenth-century house in the Algarve is a fine example of the warm earthiness and simple elegance that can be achieved using pale pinks in different textures and surfaces. Iron oxide formed the basis of the colour wash used on the wall. A stronger mix of the same colour was used for the frame of the inset Sienese fifteenth-century Madonna. The two simple stools are an old Algarvian design, while the floor is tiled with locally made clay tiles known as *ladrilhos*.

Far left The owners of this restored Yorkshire farmhouse wanted to paint their walls the colour of new pink plaster. They found it difficult to achieve. Starting with a pale neutral pink, they added yellow until at last they had created a subtle shade between pink and yellow. This tone recurs throughout the house; it flatters old wood and is comfortable to live with.

51

Left The kitchen of the Gardner-Pingree house in Salem, Massachusetts, has recently been redecorated in its original early nineteenth-century colours. The pale brown pink of the walls (once distemper – a water-based paint – now flat oil) is echoed in the deeper brick red of the chairs (which retain their original bright yellow trim) and offset by the light green woodwork. The airy feel of the room is accentuated by the scrubbed pine floor.

Above Shades of pink, mustard, brown and white are the main colours in this country drawing room. A plain French cotton was chosen not only for the elaborate curtains but also for the walls, to provide a simple background against which to display pictures and objects. The dried hydrangeas add solid touches of russet, mauve and crimson; the gypsophila makes a froth of pinky white. The white paint and the stone and porcelain vases add freshness, while the yellow chair introduces precisely the right touch of sharpness. The geometric carpet with its deep brown borders anchors the whole design. *Designer: David Hicks*

WARM PINK

These muted pinks – sometimes dirtied and matured by the addition of brown – give warmth to any room and are popular colours in vernacular interiors when they can be mixed with plaster or whitewash as well as paint. They work particularly well in dark areas where a paler pink might look washed out.

Warm pink goes well with a wide range of complementaries, both blue- and yellow-greens, as well as with related reds and browns.

It can be mixed by adding a little white to an orange-tinged earth red; add a touch of either burnt or raw umber to produce a browner, dirtied effect. Alternatively, a thin glaze of earth red can be applied over a white base and distressed – the result will look pink.

Above A wooden cupboard has been painted with a soft red glaze over a dark grey-green base. The background colour is allowed to show through, giving the paintwork richness and depth. Dull yellow ochre mouldings add definition. Inside the cupboard, a small-print paper provides a neutral backdrop for green celadon bowls and blue-and-white china plates.

Right The bedroom of this country house is given a welcoming aspect by its bold use of whites and strong but soft pink. Small touches of green, blue-green, crimson and black give definition and brightness to the overall scheme.

Below The simplicity of this eighteenth-century French bedroom has been achieved through thoughtful detailing. Four colours are used: crimson, white, brown and pink. A small-print pink wallpaper lines the walls and is the main colour in the room. It is quite a strong brown-pink, lightened by the white of the pattern. Crimson felt is used on the ceiling between the rafters to give a feeling of warmth to the room. The crimson is picked up in the trim of the muslin curtains and bed hangings, the bedlinen and in the pottery bowl. White muslin curtains diffuse the light and the highly polished wooden furniture and beams provide a solid brown framework that sets off the other colours and textures in this room.

Above Soft brown-pink is an excellent background for rich browns and reds. Here the underlying brown in the matt wall colour is picked up by the dark chocolate of the curtain fabric, the picture frame and the marble-topped table. The earthy orange-red apparent in this warm pink is echoed by the colours of the lampshade and pedestal, as well as those of the painting. The inclusion of some green in the colour scheme lends a complementary touch.

SCARLET

The brightest naturally occurring red – without a trace of blue – is scarlet, lively and exhilarating when used in interior decoration. It is an old colour – the colour of the pigments vermilion and red lead and of the dye, cochineal – which once was expensive and grand, more often employed by the artist than the house painter. But now that it is generally available, because of its warmth and almost naive quality, it is a colour sometimes associated with country and peasant interiors, red quilts and gingham fabrics.

Whether you are seeking a grand or a simple effect, this red can be effective in small quantities. As Basil Ionides, writing in 1926, suggested: 'Scarlet will rescue a dull white or cream or brown room from dullness quicker than any other colour. A line of scarlet around the panels and on the mouldings; shades of this colour on cushions; and, of course, curtains tied back with it – all these are useful.'

Red and white are an effective combination that can be enlivened by touches of bright blue and green, and gold and black. Most blues work well with red, but navy, cooler green-blues and blue-greys are generally more successful.

Above This lively fourteenth-century illustration of the Angel Gabriel, taken from an Iraqi manuscript, combines scarlet with muted shades of brown and lavender.

Right A vivid scarlet tablecloth makes a dramatic contrast with magenta flower petals in the dining room of this Mexican house. The warmth of natural wood and muted earth colours of the plastered walls softens the severe lines of the furniture.

Above Here, the stark juxtaposition of red and white benefits from careful detailing. The delicate crocheted lambrequin at this farmhouse window links the red woodwork with the uneven white plasterwork. The green tulip leaves provide a splash of contrast.

Left Vibrant reds predominate in this sitting room. The scarlet of the door and the walls of the hallway was achieved by covering a salmon pink oil-based undercoat with two coats of rose madder glaze. The red is continued in the two rich reds of the sofa tartan and in the red stripe of the tartan carpet. The pale yellow ochre glaze on the sitting room walls makes a neutral, warm background. *Owners/designers: Annie and Lachlan Stewart*

COOL RED

The cool reds – those that have blue in them – include shades of crimson, raspberry and cerise. Crimson is the colour of the organic pigment produced from carmine, the red dye that comes from cochineal. Like scarlet, it is an old, once extremely expensive, colour.

Carmine lake pigment, mixed with varying amounts of white and blue, would have been the basis of most of the cool reds, pinks and purples used in painting grand houses until the synthesis of mauve, magenta and crimson between 1856 and 1869.

The cool reds can seem thin and hard, unless handled with care. At their best, however, they are rich and vital.

The complementary of crimson is a yellow-green. This contrast can seem too brilliant but if the green is knocked back slightly, they look good together. The deeper shades of crimson are more purplish than brown, and light and dark shades harmonize well.

Splashes of crimson also go well with violet, and warm yellow and orange bring out its blueness. Blue makes it seem more orange.

Three studies in crimson and green. In the fresh, light room (**above**) the colours have been knocked back to soften the contrast. The colours in the view from the hallway of a London restaurant (**right**) are much more intense, yet the effect is dramatic without being dazzling: the paintwork is saturated mid green but the red wall fabric is slightly muted in its colour and softened still further by its moiré texture and pattern of gold medallions. In the eighteenth-century bedroom (**far right**), the original deep blue-grey green paintwork offsets the bright bedspread.

DEEP RED

The richest of the reds, deep red is the colour of garnets and black cherries.

Based on crimson, it was an expensive colour until the synthesis of alizarin crimson in 1868. Victorian house painters then mixed crimson with burnt sienna and blue to produce a deep maroon. The colour was often combined in early Victorian interiors with deep blue and rich chocolate brown paint. Now, deep red is popular in a brighter form, more akin to old red lacquer.

It is an intriguing colour, with cool and warm aspects, and works especially well when used as a wall colour or when incorporated in a mixture of other rich colours and patterns. The complementary of this deep red is olive green. Artificial light emphasizes its warmth, making it a good choice for dining rooms and rooms that are used for entertaining. It is a complex colour, benefiting from the addition of other pigments – and it is not difficult to mix. A little burnt sienna or burnt umber will make it earthier and browner, raw umber will age it and ultramarine will make it colder and more violet.

Left This eclectic arrangement of oriental fabrics and artefacts was inspired by a trip to Katmandu and northern India. Colour is the unifying element that holds this profusion of fascinating objects together. And the plain painted chest of drawers provides an important focus in a room where all the surfaces – including the ceiling – are covered with densely patterned materials.

Above This country dining room is a careful balance of ivory white and deep red. The room receives little sunshine during the day but it is always bright and welcoming, and at night its atmosphere is warm and rich. The burnt orange and browns in the carpet, the vermilion chair and the brown kashmir paisley tablecloth reflect the subtle mixture of colours that contribute to this scheme.

To achieve a similar wall colour and finish, apply a base colour of bright red, a second coat of carefully blended deep red glaze and a top coat of matt varnish tinted with burnt umber. *Designer: Merlin Pennink*

Right The walls of this library are lined with books with the exception of an area above the mantelpiece. The piece of silk velvet which fits this space was taken from a Victorian evening skirt. The fabric catches the light, making a lively backdrop to the picture and objects on and above the mantelpiece. The atmosphere is one of intimacy and relaxation. *Designer: David Hicks*

Left In the winter living room of a large farmhouse, antique fabrics rather than paint have been used to introduce the colour. The textures of plush and velvet add warmth and richness to the purplish reds and brownish crimsons; roughly plastered walls and coir matting provide a cool, neutral background. Dark green provides a lively note of contrast; black and gold complete the colour picture.

The deep-buttoned chest is covered in a luxurious flat red velvet, the sofa in Victorian chintz and the large armchair against the window in a French brocade. The other two armchairs and the low, long footstool are upholstered in cut velvet. *Designer/ antiques: Andrea de Montal. Upholsterer: Paul Harrison*

Above left This panelled Manhattan dining room was dragged and then sponged a dark lacquer red. The purple-brown carpet anchors the design and the intense red of the coasters, candles and chair trimmings provides the highlights. A second colour, a warm yellow-brown, has been used on the upholstery and in the marbling on the cornice and skirting. *Designer: Mark Hampton*

Above right Deep violet-brown walls make this large room appear welcoming and intimate. The same warm, advancing colour is picked up in the painting, the oriental carpet and the furnishing fabrics, while a cool contrast is provided by the blue-green leather of the chairs and the metallic glitter of the unusual silver lampshades. *Designer: Hamoush Bowler*

SOFT RED & PINK

The bluish reds, when muted, seem to lose some of their coldness and become almost warm and faded in appearance. They can introduce an element of grandeur to a room, but they are warm and comforting colours, pleasant and easy to live with.

Fresh, sharp or acid colours are difficult to combine with these soft reds and pinks; natural and neutral colours – whites, creams and magnolias – can add freshness, while greens can act as a complement and contrast. Greys and browns can also work well in conjunction with them. Touches of colour on the same side of the spectrum – crimsons, terracottas and pinks – are effective when used alongside them, particularly when offset by cool greens. Pinks and soft reds make good wall colours and translate well in fabric form, particularly in cotton, linen and taffeta.

Left Red-and-white checked and striped fabrics echo the pinky red border of this elegantly simple eighteenth-century Swedish bedroom. The soft reds complement the muted wood tones and the pale green of the walls and chairs.

Above This end of the hall in an English country house has been decorated in a lively and robust manner. The stone flagged floor and uneven plaster walls provide a cool framework which needs strong, slightly warmer colours to complement it. The walls have been enhanced by a glaze of raw umber and white to give a stone effect. The fabric of the armchair and settle introduces two shades of red – a soft red and a deeper crimson – colours which are reinforced by the Turkey rug and the red panel of the cushions. Touches of complementary green complete the picture. *Designer: Merlin Pennink*

Right These fabrics show the softness and strength of just a few shades of soft red used in juxtaposition with neutrals or with a touch of black detail. The colours are subtly enlivened by pattern, even in the simplest form.

Left An underlying bluish red hue links many of the decorative elements in this room in the Gran Canaria. Think of the pale cyclamen pink of the walls as a tint of the colour, the blotting paper pink of the sofa as a muted tone and the burgundy of the velvet corner chair as a very deep shade and you will see why everything works together so well. Even the blue-grey dragged paintwork of the doorway and the dado rail is slightly tinged with pink. The other colours in the room are the faded sea green of the shutters and the silvery blue of the chair upholstered in Fortuny cotton. *Owner/designer: Christophe Gollut*

Right Offset by the muted grey-greens and natural wood colours at Lebell Manor in Finland, a subtle rose pink infuses the room with soft colour. Most striking in the panel borders and valance, the pink is also picked up in the patterns of the upholstery fabric.

BLUE-RED

A vibrant, intense, saturated purplish blue-red was first made available in the 1860s as a result of the synthesis of the new dye, fuschine. The English called the new colour magenta after the Battle of Magenta (1859). In 1935, the master publicist, Schiaparelli, called a bright but not so deep or purple version of the colour 'shocking pink'.

It is a strong, demanding colour that needs careful handling in order to draw out its most attractive characteristics. Small amounts work well with touches of other equally vibrant, hot or acidic colours – turquoise, peacock blue, tangerine, or strong lemon yellow and lime green.

The colour is often associated with the diaphanous silks, saris and embroidered sequined cloths of Far Eastern countries.

Above The dark panelling in this house in Thailand makes a striking background for brightly coloured silk cushions. The magenta is not overpowered by the other equally vibrant colours.

Left The matt Indian cotton fabric that covers the sofas is of a soft magenta that harmonizes well with the soft browns, dusty pinks and oranges of the cushions. The patterned fabrics on the chair and the sofa cushions introduce acid yellow, sharp green, vermilion and aquamarine and keep the composition lively. *Designer: John Stefanidis*

Far left The cherry coloured sofa, bright pink wallpaper patterned with black-and-white prints and the deep brown taffeta curtains, unlined and almost translucent, all share the same underlying hue. The melon-coloured silk and the embroidered scarlet Indian cloth that cover the chairs provide splashes of strong colour while the carpet introduces yellow, pink and white in a small geometric pattern. *Designer: David Hicks*

VIOLET & PURPLE

Covering the spectrum of colours from intense purple to mauves, pale lilacs and violets, these hues vary according to their proximity to blue or red and their degree of tone and intensity.

Since earliest times, purple has been linked with majesty and power. In the West it was also the colour of mourning. In 1856, Perkin brought in mauve – a synthetic, organic dye – and it became a popular colour with the Victorians.

Because of its intensity, purple is most effective as a detail in a room – in fabrics or on objects. The paler mauves, violets and lilacs are easier to use over large areas and they work well with varying shades of green.

Few natural purple pigments exist, so the colour is usually made by mixing blue and red. Reds that veer towards blue and warm blues will produce the best results – cool colours give a violet-brown.

Left Violet is perhaps a surprising colour choice for a kitchen but the shades used here create a fresh, clean, functional effect which is offset by the crisp white of the china and of the room's detailing. The ceramic tiles are in a harmonious range of warm and cool mauves and violets.

Above This simply-furnished bedroom in Connecticut, combining antique and modern elements, is given an arresting and unusual twist by the choice of violet for the cotton-covered walls and ceiling and the lacquered tub table. Infrequently used as an overall decorating colour – particularly in bedrooms – violet has a startlingly fresh appeal.
Designer: John Saladino

Right Pale violet provides a tranquil background colour for the rich arrangement of objects and furniture in the 'Justice Room' at Sir Sacheverell Sitwell's former home. A pair of black lacquered cabinets and a glass dome, displaying stuffed birds, are set alongside statues and elaborate mirror and picture frames. The white-painted door, with its unusual red-glass windows, contrasts with the pale violet wall panels framed with decorative black-edged floral borders. The black in the room – offset by gold detailing – has a strength which balances the red of the glass while the white softens and adds delicacy to the violet.

Left This is a fine illustration of the impact of splashes of colour set against neutral tones. Rather than existing as a permanent feature of the decoration, here colour is introduced by way of such ephemeral features as scarves, dressing gowns, flowers and pictures. A range of blue-reds is combined in this bedroom – from plum, crimson, magenta and purplish red through to violet.

Left The warm purple colour of the dresser provides a fine focus for this kitchen and an excellent setting for a collection of blue china and assorted glassware. The brownish yellow of the tea caddy and the green of the tray and glasses create a split complementary scheme. The silver-grey of the pewter plates makes the purple appear brighter while the warm wood of the furniture and floorboards draws out its redness.

Right A cool colour scheme has been created in the attic bedroom of this Rome apartment: the pale green of the eighteenth-century Piedmontese wood-panelled walls acts as the background colour to an imposing bed draped in mauve-patterned *toile de Jouy*. The two colours are picked up in the Aubusson carpet which, with its blue background, is the deepest hue in the room. Bleached rustic beams make an important contribution to the atmosphere that combines simplicity, luxuriousness and intimacy. *Designer: Karl Lagerfeld*

BLUE

WARM BLUE

These intense strong blues are saturated colours – neither tinted with white nor dulled with complementary umber.

The colour was obtained originally from natural ultramarine, manufactured from the semi-precious stone lapis lazuli, introduced into Europe as a pigment in the twelfth century. It was so expensive, however, that its use was confined mainly to picture painting. It was not

Above In the collection of decorative Victorian art created by Charles and Lavinia Handley-Read, intense blue provides a background that sets off the contrasting colours of the tiles and centre plate; it also balances the intensity of the patterned wallpaper in high Victorian fashion.

Left The strong saturated blue of this stairway in Jodhpur, northwest India, is brought out by the intense but muted turquoise of the door.

Far left The entrance hall of this house in County Donegal, Ireland, has been painted an electrifying blue. The intense colour was achieved by mixing 'Reckitt's Blue' laundry aid – a strong blue powder – with a distemper-like base. This was painted directly on to the plaster to give an uneven, powdery finish. The same colour was later reapplied using a more stable, transparent acrylic base. Touches of white offset the vibrant blue. No other colours are necessary.
Designer: Derek Hill

until 1828 that an artificial ultramarine was made available and probably not until the mid years of that century that the pigment was used in house painting. Cobalt blue, slightly less red, was also an early nineteenth-century discovery.

The depth of these blues makes them a good choice for the walls of a small dark room. Used as a wall colour in a large room, the colour works well if broken up by pictures and ornate mirrors. These blues are effective when offset by white, gold or yellow or when combined with strong reds or orange.

Right A warm intense blue, mixed from French ultramarine and cobalt, has been used to paint this wall-niche. The colour provides an effective background for a collection of blue-and-white china. *Designer: Annie Sloan*

Below The richness of colour and flatness of texture of these terracotta jars provide an ideal complement to the rich blue of the rough-surfaced wall behind. Both are strong, uncomplicated colours and the absence of other hues gives this composition great strength.

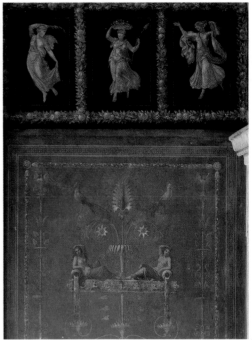

Above This detail from the frescoed portico of Schinkel's Schloss Charlottenhof in Potsdam, East Germany, shows the influence of classical colour and design on early nineteenth-century European interiors. A reinterpretation of a wall at Pompeii, the saturated, warm blue of the panel is drawn out by a red band of similar tone and is offset by delicate gold coloured detailing. A similar luminous quality could be achieved by painting a pure deep cobalt blue pigment – bound with egg-yolk – over a ground of brilliant white gesso. This white ground acts as a back light, brightening the colour without reducing its intensity.

Left A strong pure blue is used in this modern passageway to add a softening note of colour amid the rigid geometric lines and hard white surfaces. The blue finds a complementary echo in the reddish brown of the brick ceiling and the floor.

DEEP WARM BLUE

These soft, deep and sometimes luminous blues recall the colour of a dark night sky. Although too muted to be bright, they nevertheless have strength and are tinged with red's warming influence.

The potency and depth of these blues are reminiscent of the ancient colour that was obtained from the leaves of the indigo plant. The Romans called the dye '*color indicus*' – literally, the colour from India – and, indeed, most of the indigo that was imported into Europe from the eighteenth century on was shipped by the British East India Company.

In the nineteenth century, using natural dyes such as indigo, William Morris reproduced a wide range of blues – including a deep warm blue – in his chintz and wallpaper designs.

This blue, whose complementary is deep orange, can provide a fine background for other strong colours. Reds can look particularly lustrous against it, while white will provide a crisp, striking contrast. Brighter, lighter and sharper colours can lend it sparkle.

Above This vaulted ceiling at the top of a spiral staircase in a converted church has been painted with deep dark blue and speckled with white stars. The depth of the blue creates the effect of a never-ending vault of night sky. A narrow border of complementary pale orange makes the colour appear more vibrant. *Designer: Roy Grant*

Left The deep blue striped wallpaper used in this sitting room works well as a background for the hot, bright reds and oranges of the soft furnishings. This particular blue has nothing of the chilliness characteristic of several other blues and its capacity for considerable warmth has been drawn out skilfully in the powerful colour scheme. *Designer: David Hicks*

Far left The unadorned walls of this Swedish farmhouse have been painted deep reddish blue. The colour not only links the adjoining rooms but also emphasizes the subtlety of the bleached boards of the floor and ceiling and the richness of the yellow runners.

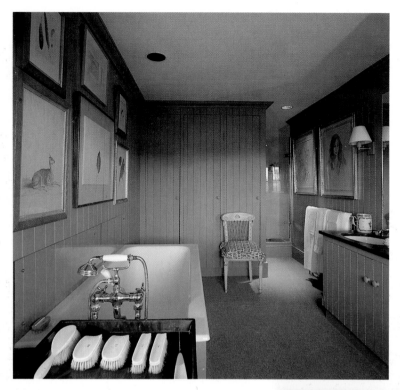

Above Here, a clean, intense soft blue, with no hint of green, together with the textures of the panelled walls and fittings, creates a bright, fresh atmosphere. *Designer: Piers von Westenholz*

Above right Large areas of this bedroom are without colour – white walls and bedlinen, grey floor tiles, brown furnishings – yet the space is made cheerful by subtle touches of warm, advancing red and blue. The blue of the bedstead contains enough white to make it bright and not too dark or pale a tone. The vibrant red, blue and white of the picture draws the scheme together.

Right The faded blue cotton chair covers in this spacious country drawing room give a light, summery feel that contrasts with the warm mellow browns of the brick floor and oak beams. *Designer: John Stefanidis*

LIGHT WARM BLUE

The colour of hyacinths, campanulas and cornflowers, these light warm blues are gentle, soothing, welcoming and easy to live with. They work effectively with a wide range of other colours such as: complementary orange, shades of terracotta, yellows, reds and lilac. Greens of similar tone can establish a striking contrast, while white teams especially well with them. The soft warm blues are highly versatile and adaptable colours, suitable for houses of many different types, styles and periods and for all rooms, whatever their function.

These blues can be mixed from either cobalt or ultramarine and white: cobalt with white produces the purest and most intense of this range of colours. A touch of complementary unber produces a cooler, cloudier effect.

Above Blue and white always work well together. These weathered, faded shutters at the Schloss Charlottenhof preserve a distinctiveness by virtue of their simple design and tonal contrast – muted mid blue and chalky white.

Left The owners of this house in London's Spitalfields chose their wall colour after reading that blue was often used for kitchens in the eighteenth century – it was thought to repel flies. The three primaries work together in the colour scheme. When used in the same degrees of intensity, they tend to cancel each other out but here, the blues are soft, the reds brownish, with just a hint of yellow in the tartan tiles surrounding the black coal-fired Victorian stove.

The clear, textural blue of the rough plastered walls was achieved by colour-washing a pure cobalt-blue pigment in a transparent scumble glaze over a matt white oil-based undercoat. The paintwork was given a final coat of matt varnish.
Owners/designers: Annie and Lachlan Stewart

Above The soft, muted matt blue in this Irish bedroom contrasts with the white of the fireplace, chair and ceiling. The white serves to reflect light on to the walls, giving a gentle, restful effect. Touches of red – in the chair fabric, large painting and mahogany chest of drawers – add warmth to the room.

To achieve this muted blue, mix cobalt blue and white knocked back with either raw or burnt umber.

Right Widely differing colours can be used together harmoniously. The colour scheme of this bedroom combines blue, green and pink in almost exactly the same tones.

A Moroccan artist's powder pigment, bound with milk, was applied as a very watery wash over a base coat of white to achieve a misty, soothing effect. *Artist: Amanda Feilding*

BRIGHT BLUE

Recalling the clean, clear colour of a cloudless summer sky, the bright blues are characterized by their depth and intensity and have a long history in interior house painting and decoration.

In the early sixteenth century, bright blue was a popular ceiling colour. Madame de Rombouillet used the same shade in her famous 'chambre bleu' in Paris in the 1620s: here, the velvet hangings – patterned in gold – the chairs, the table-carpet and the painted walls were all blue. A similar opulent effect using this vivid blue was achieved in the dining room at Ham House near Richmond in the late 1630s.

Bright blue works well with orange, natural and neutral tones, white and mid greens and looks especially striking offset by gold detailing.

Above Several blues can be used together in the same scheme without appearing discordant, as shown in this house in Oyster Bay outside New York. Here, the greenish blue of the walls provides a rich background for a bright blue bench and a grey-blue horse. All the colours are of a similar intensity and so achieve tonal harmony. *Designer: Barry Ferguson*

Right Three shades of bright blue are offset by the natural golden pinewood stairs in this old farmhouse in Sweden. Mix ultramarine and cerulean pigments with oil, turpentine and zinc white and apply on to plaster walls to achieve this textural effect. *Owner/designer: Yvonne Schmitterlöw*

Far right Inspired by an illustration in a history of Cardinal Richelieu written by Leloire, this imaginative bedroom uses gold detailing against a predominance of intense bright blue. The golden tones of the headboard are picked up by the more earthy yellows used in the pictures and on the ceiling. The richness of the wall colour is countered by a blue-and-white bedspread and by the strong geometric floor tiles.

DEEP COOL BLUE

Deep cool blue is a very dark greenish blue, a distinctive colour, often associated with the blues of military uniform and cavalry jackets.

The colour can be mixed from Prussian blue – a compound of ferric ferrocyanide – which was the first synthetic pigment ever to be produced. Although discovered by Diesbach in Berlin at the beginning of the eighteenth century, the pigment was not made available until the 1720s.

In the art world, Georges Braque employed this deep cool blue as a contrasting tone to rich red-browns. Picasso, during his 'Blue Period', used it to create atmospheres of melancholy and introspection.

Deep cool blue works well with oranges, reds, pinks, yellows and terracottas. The colour can look particularly striking when offset by white or when combined with touches of gilt or gold. Small amounts of shocking pink, lime green or turquoise look eyecatching against the darkest of deep cool blues.

Above A fourteenth-century Chinese porcelain dish combining deep blue and white.

Left Changes in colour from one room to another can be handled in various ways. Here, dark, green-touched blues give on to the pale, but related greenish blues of the hallway. The deep blue doorframe, surrounded by a blue of a slightly lighter tone, draws the eye through to the brighter colours beyond.

Far left The Tent Room at Schloss Charlottenhof, designed in the late 1820s, draws upon the decorative simplicity characteristic of the Napoleonic military style popular in France at the beginning of the nineteenth century. A deep cool blue, accented against white, creates a scheme of exceptional elegance. The cotton-covered campaign chairs and beds are echoed in the matching paper of the walls and pitched ceiling; the warmer hues of the simple wooden floorboards add lightness as well as a contrast of colour and texture. The strong stripes and the contours of the draped fabrics give depth and dimension to the room.

Above Printed and patterned fabrics in blues, cream and gold.

Left Colour and design hold equal precedence in this dining room. A wall of cool dark blue contrasts with the cream of the inset panels and ceiling. The gold panel frames, with the tones of the wooden floor, table and cupboard offset the coolness of the blue and cream.

Right A similar combination of colours is put to use in a more formal setting in the drawing room at Edgewater, near the Hudson River. The deep blue fabric, grey walls and stone-effect wall panels contrast with the warmer, reddish brown of the wood. The elegant French Empire-style chairs and sofa are complemented by the rich blue and golden yellow upholstery with its 'Napoleonic Bee' design. The combination of blue and gold is echoed in the fine china.

GREY-BLUE

The grey-blues are a subtle, delicate and sophisticated range of colours, some of which have a slight greenish tinge. They have become associated with a style of decorating characterized by restrained elegance, charm and an atmosphere of airy lightness.

These subdued blues have a long tradition of use in domestic interior decoration and are often associated with the muted colours used in seventeenth-century Colonial Williamsburg in Virginia, where they were applied to cover walls as well as furniture and exterior and interior woodwork. Grey-blues were also much used in both simple and grand interiors in late eighteenth-century Sweden.

Perhaps the most famous colour developed by the neo-classical pottery

Above Grey-blue wallpaper – pale blue with a deeper blue design – acts as an excellent background for this distinctive bathroom. It provides a muted complement to the orange tints in the pictures and fabrics as well as a tonal link with the pine wash-stand – hand-painted in blue watercolours – and the bright cobalt blue of the chinaware.

Left The muted grey-blue used on the walls of this English country drawing room is one of the colours in the range of Wedgwood blues. The same blue could be made up using cobalt and white, knocked back with a little burnt umber.

Far left The panelled walls of this Georgian dining room have been colour-washed using a pale eau de nil emulsion (water-based paint) tinted with strong blue and a touch of umber. The scheme is drawn together by the dark turquoise of the silk-covered chairs and the strong blues and reds of the crewelwork tablecloth; the caramel and browns of the nineteenth-century watercolour fabric designs are echoed in the oak ceiling beams. *Designer/antiques: Andrea de Montal. Artist: Josephine Hensser*

manufacturer Josiah Wedgwood was a clear grey-blue, still known today as Wedgwood Blue.

Colour schemes based on grey- and greeny grey-blue are often delicate and light-enhancing. The subtlety of the colour means that it is often best used in simple schemes. It works happily with harmonious combinations of white and cream, oyster and terracotta; deeper tones of blue or green, and perhaps a touch of coral, provide good accents. It is particularly effective with natural wood tones, highlighting their warm hints of orange with its own complementary blueness. Grey-blue or greeny grey-blue can also be used as a near neutral background for touches of brighter colour – for vibrant reds and oranges, for example.

Above Colour has been used sparingly in the dining room of this eighteenth-century house in New England. Beyond the shades of white and wood, the only colour in the room is provided by the deep greeny grey-blue window frames which echo the steel-grey tones of the antique French metal chairs. This touch of colour gives a subtle warmth to an otherwise cool interior.

Right This scheme shows how our eyes pick up even quite faint colour if it is set beside its complementary. The warm orange-browns of the wood floor and wall draw out the soft blue-grey stain on the cupboard.

Far right The elegant grey-blue of the panelled walls in this Swedish summer guest house epitomizes simplicity and restraint. An unadorned window makes the most of the available light, allowing it to filter gently on to a bare bleached floor and cool white-painted furniture; a touch of colour is added in the striped chair covers.

GREEN-BLUE

Cool and elegant, the green-blues are reminiscent of the faded aquamarine of tropical seas or the delicate tint of birds' eggs. They are ambiguous colours, on the border between green and blue.

Although pale, they can possess some of the intensity of turquoise – if dirtied with burnt sienna or umber, a softer effect is achieved. At their most translucent, they lend airiness to interior schemes; in more muted, matt or grey tones they have a subtle 'period' feel.

At Colonial Williamsburg in Virginia, a pale greenish blue, known as apothecary blue, was much used alongside pale rose, tallow gold and pewter grey. In the 1820s, the designer Karl Friedrich Schinkel used a distinctive blue-green on the alderwood sofa and walls of the sitting room at Schloss Charlottenhof, East Germany.

The way in which we perceive the

Above This simple attic room has been painted in a very pale greenish blue, with a lighter tone used on the panels of the cupboard for depth and dimension. The wooden shelves, stripped woodwork around the window and varnished plaster at the back of the cupboard offset the cold, clean wall colour with their warm, rough textures.

Right A clear and modern ambience is achieved in this dining room with its pale but vibrant greeny blue walls and warm orange-red rug. The dark green window frames and strong blue sofa cushions give weight to the scheme.

Far right The cool green-blue on the walls of this London sitting room was chosen as a foil for the reddish orange of the beaten copper fireplace. The room's details have been picked out in four shades of the green-blue, the lightest on the ceiling, the darkest on the cupboard panels. The blue and green elements in the wall colour are echoed in the carpet and mid-green sofa.

green-blues is influenced considerably by their surrounding colours: adjacent oranges or browns tend to give emphasis to the complementary blue aspect of the mix; while, if set against red or pink, the green bias of the colour becomes more pronounced. As a cool colour, greeny blue often works well with warmer shades such as soft pinks, terracottas, and hot spicy gingers.

Above This panelled and curtainless dining room in an eighteenth-century house overlooking Clapham Common in London achieves an airy period elegance. The pale green-blue of the walls was inspired by the interior colours used in Williamsburg, Virginia. It has been painted up over the cornice to give the room more height. *Designer: Miranda Humphries*

Far left and left This dining room re-uses canvas panels painted originally by Rex Whistler in 1937 for an apartment in London. The pictures are painted in *grisaille*, using black, white and grey shades to imitate the style of a mezzotint. The shimmering silver gives a textural effect. Beside so much intricate monochrome, the cool greeny blue of the background area, chairbacks and tablecloth adds a welcome touch of colour. *Designer: David Hicks*

Above Colour ideas can often be drawn from nature's striking colour combinations. These blackbird's eggs are speckled with ginger dots, a natural complement to the green-blue.

GREEN

Right The panelled walls of the upstairs landing of the Tudor manor house, Dorney Court, have been painted a deep turquoise. The colour provides a lively background for the pictures and a pleasing contrast to the warm, reddish tones of the old wood and the deep terracotta border of the painted flower-panel set into the wall.

Below A similar combination of colours, textures and materials is used at Mount Vernon, Virginia – a late eighteenth-century house, former residence of George Washington. A turquoise door makes a block of strong colour against the white walls and wooden floorboards. The oil lamp with its mirrored background is edged in a paler version of the door colour, providing a link with the room's two dominant colour elements of turquoise and white.

BLUE-GREEN

The blue-greens cover a wider band of the spectrum than any other range of colours. Turquoise is the general name used to describe the most intense hues which are on the border between blue and green, although it remains a subject of debate as to exactly which colour turquoise is: to some it appears blue, to others green.

The precious stone, originally imported by the Egyptians from Sinai, provides only a very loose colour guide since, depending on its quality, it can vary considerably between blue and green. This colour range is often associated with the ancient cultures of Peru, Tibet, Egypt and Persia. Inspirational colour schemes using

Above Bright, richly textured fabrics – here combining turquoise with orange-reds – can add life and sparkle to a room.

Left In this small, recessed room the distinctive turquoise of antique Islamic and Persian ceramics is offset by white paintwork and by a vibrant wall colour of orange-yellow. The colour scheme – with its touches of red – gives a cosy intimacy to the room. Turquoise was used extensively in countries such as Iran which once had to transport water into the desert from the sea – reproduced in objects, such as these ceramics, the colour was a constant reminder of both water and the sky. *Designer: Hamoush Bowler*

Below The matt blue-green of this Cotswold dining room was achieved by the traditional technique of limewashing: unpigmented limewash is first applied to a lime plaster then pure ground pigments are mixed into slaked lime and painted on. The resulting colour has great freshness and clarity.
Architect: Andrew Townsend

blue-greens can be found in the murals, ceramics, carpets and decorative objects of these ancient cultures. Blue-greens combined with deep reds, deep blues, whites, orange, ochre yellows, rust and sometimes mauve and maroon, produced rich, warm schemes.

Influenced by Persian colours, the Arts and Crafts ceramist William de Morgan made considerable use of turquoise – often placed with deep blues and greens in many of his late nineteenth-century designs. In Art Deco and Art Nouveau interiors, pale, neutral colours – whites,

creams and beiges – would often be offset by touches of pale blue-greens or turquoise used alongside warm yellows, orange and sometimes even lime green. Blue-green teamed with orange was also popular in the 1960s.

Simple, more subtle, colour schemes can be achieved using pale blue-greens with neutrals, white and black.

Turquoise pigment remains expensive but the colour can also be mixed very successfully from a blue-green, such as phthalocyanine, with cerulean blue and a touch of white.

Below An imposing antique chair sets the tone for the corner of a newly decorated dining room in a London flat. The blue-green of the self-patterned upholstery cotton works well with the muted version of the same colour in the wall painting. The pitted surface and dirtied pink of the original 100-year-old plaster dull down the brightness of fresh paint and lend an antique look to this classical setting. *Designer: Diana Nicol*

Above In many rooms, colour is provided by the walls. Here, however, the wallpaper is neutral and colour is introduced by way of the furnishings and fabrics. Subtle tints of pale blue-green predominate: on the sofa covers, china borders, lampshades and picture mounts. These light, cool tones are offset by the dark, rich, more spicy reds and browns of the carpet, cushions and wooden side tables. *Designer: Merlin Pennink*

DARK GREEN

The deep muted greens are the colour of holly, ivy and fir trees. Popular colour names include forest and bottle green.

Green has long been a widely used decorating colour and until the early eighteenth century was probably mixed from the pigment verdigris, if an oil paint was wanted, or green verditer for a distemper. Both of these greens have a bluish tinge and verdigris tends to darken with age. Early-eighteenth-century panelling that retains its original oil paint looks much darker now than when it was first painted. In the seventeenth century, dark green was sometimes offset with gilt or gold detailings and mouldings. Deep green, along with other muted colours, was also popular in the Victorian period when it was called Brunswick green.

The dark greens have a dramatic quality when used on walls, where they work well in a matt or eggshell (flat or mid-sheen) finish. A dark green wall needs strong wall light to ensure that the green does not sink into a black.

Dark green works well with scarlet, crimson, orange-red and brown-pink – as well as with pale and dark yellow and bright blue.

Left The decorator's brief for this small dark basement room was to create a rich Gothic ambience.

A dark green was chosen for the walls and ceiling; the colour was made up from thin layers of deep green and cobalt blue glaze over a pale apricot eggshell ground. A glaze of Prussian green and indigo was added for the final coat.

The design of the frieze (**above**) was created by scratching through to the eggshell base with a sharp blade. The scalloped border was painted in a yellow-ochre glaze and then distressed. Stripes of dark green, dark red and yellow ochre decorate the cornice and doorframe. The deep green walls turn a dark inky colour in the soft warm light of candles, giving an air of mystery to the room while the frieze sparkles as the light reveals different colours. *Artist: Lucy Spagnol*

Right Dark blue-greens – in the chintz bed-head, antique French quilt, what-not and Italian chair – are combined with white and cream in this bedroom to create a smart, crisp effect. A gentle light filtering through the shutters softens the atmosphere. *Designer: Diana Griffin-Strauss*

GREY-GREEN

The grey-greens are the colours of the willow, the silvery side of the olive leaf and of the distinctive glaze of the Chinese porcelain first made during the Sung period (tenth to thirteenth centuries AD). The colour, like the glaze, is often called celadon – a name which is thought to be derived from the shepherd called Céladon in D'Urfé's pastoral, *L'Astrée*, who was wan faced and wore green clothes. Celadon ware varies in colour from a transparent olive to a milky sea green, while what is now generally referred to as celadon green is a paler, greyer shade.

The grey-greens, popular on both sides of the Atlantic in the 1700s, are not intense colours but soft, cool and muted. They work well with all natural colours – the browns, ochres and creams – and can also provide a neutral background for very strong colours, for orange, purple and peacock blue, or for complementary shades such as dirty pink or crimson.

Below The Gardner-Pingree House in Salem, Massachusetts, built by the architect Samuel McIntyre in 1804–6, has been carefully restored as a fine example of the American Federal style. The pale, greyish green of the woodwork harmonizes with the equally pale pink of the upper walls, providing a light but restrained background for the dark blue-and-white gingham bed hanging.

Below The walls of this bedroom in Manhattan are lined with Chinese patterned wallpaper: against a background of celadon green – a colour also shown in the pottery **(right)** – *grisaille* peony trees predominate with occasional brightly coloured birds and butterflies. Grey-green *faille* has been chosen for the fabrics with antique and modern off-white lace and linen. White-painted furniture, white lampshades, glass and silverware all add to the room's delicate effect. *Designer: Mark Hampton*

BRIGHT GREEN

This strong intense hue is the colour of emeralds, polished apples and new grass.

Bright, vibrant green was a popular colour for fabrics, curtains and bed hangings in the seventeenth and early eighteenth centuries.

Its subsequent use in decoration is closely linked to the discovery of chrome yellow, whose manufacture at the end of the eighteenth century made the first stable bright greens available. It is not surprising, therefore, that the great age of bright green was the Empire period. Napoleon, who had the shade of Empire green fixed by decree, favoured the colour for his state apartments and used it boldly with white and gold.

Bright greens also work well with vivid yellows, ochres and gold, and pale and dark shades of greenish blue. Muted crimsons and pinks can provide a soft contrast.

Above Broad areas of bright and deep green, highlighted by a splash of red-patterned tartan rug, give this small bedroom a rich yet soothing intimacy.

Left This lavishly adorned bedroom combines bright green-patterned fabric on the walls with a faded green-patterned Persian carpet – the original inspiration for the room. The brightness of the fabric is broken up not only by the gold-framed eighteenth-century paintings but also by the large arabesque motif printed in red and pale turquoise. The nineteenth-century Bokhara bedcover provides a large area of complementary red. *Designer: Michael Szell*

Far left An austere, neo-classical bedroom designed by Karl Friedrich Schinkel mixes bright green, gold and white in Napoleonic style. There is no pattern in the room apart from the elaborate curtain fringes; the design relies on strong colour and the modelling of the space. The precise white detailing gives the room a modern feel.

Above Glazed earthenware pots of soft green provide a restrained focus for this modern interior. The matt white paintwork allows the full subtlety of the colour to be appreciated. The 1930s pots were designed by Keith Murray for Wedgwood.

Right The spacious Victorian verandah that surrounds Nindooinbah House, near Brisbane, has been painted in traditional colours of green, tan and cream. The furnishings add deeper shades of green and brown, but the whole effect is cool and airy, echoing the lush foliage of the garden.

MUTED GREEN

The soft, muted greens are natural,
comforting, restful colours, evocative of
summer leaves and grass. The human eye
adjusts easily to green: it does not seem to
advance or to recede or to appear
overwhelmingly cold or warm, even
though the more muted greens have a
slightly cool bias.

Muted greens were popular in the
eighteenth century and are often
associated with the Scottish architect,
Robert Adam. The same colours were
also used on painted Regency chairs.

Muted green works well with deep,
muted and pale versions of its
complementary, red. Drawing
inspiration from the natural landscape,
one can see that many greens are striking
used in combination.

Above The simple green-and-white checks —
of two different sizes — used in this modern
Swedish bedroom were inspired by the
traditional eighteenth-century fabrics of
Gripsholm Castle. They provide a strong but
uncomplicated foil for the intricate
wallpaper, which is composed of eighteenth-
century botanical prints protected by a
yellowed varnish.

The dado and cornice, in a muted earth
green colour, bridge the gap between the
colours of the wall and the bed hangings.

Right The green of the leaves in this early
nineteenth-century paper used in a town
house in Salem, Massachusetts, has been
subdued by the pattern so that the overall
effect is of a soft grey-green paper that
merges well with the pale grey paintwork.
The white, black and gold of the chair, table
and mirror look bright and well-defined in
contrast.

LIGHT GREEN

Often compared to the colour of the almond-tree leaf or of pistachio, light green is any green that contains white. Until this century, there were few permanent green pigments. The most usual were those that could be extracted from natural sources – from copper and green earth.

The versatility and subtlety of the light greens make them extremely effective in decoration. They can act as a successful foil to many other colours and are at their most elegant when working with cream, ivory, white and ochre-yellows. The greens in this range that are slightly more blue work well with green- and grey-blues. Strawberry, shell or dusty, matt pinks and terracottas make a particularly effective contrast to the light mid greens.

The colour may be made from a green pigment or dye, or from a mixture of yellow and blue. The addition of white produces a number of effects: a small amount of white will make the colour opaque but the green will retain its brightness; a lot of white will give the green a soft, powdery look.

Above The light, natural colours of the wood-panelled floor and ceiling of this eighteenth-century Finnish manor house provide an ideal context for the green of the wall. The combination of light green with the hint of faded blue on the canopied bed produces a particularly harmonious and restful effect. And the beautifully simple lines and colours of the bed itself are complemented by the more ornate decorative details in the room.

Right An eccentric arch, created entirely in paint, changes the shape and atmosphere of this simple bedroom. The wall colour of dry pistachio is complemented by the rosy colour and rich texture of the bedcovering. The result is an example of how a good idea, carried out with flair and bravado, can transform a room.

Above The contrasting colours of light green and off-white are shown at their most elegant in these fine examples of Federal-style painted columns and panels at Homewood House in Baltimore.

Left A house in Marrakesh, characterized by traditional fretwork, again displays how the most simple of colour ideas can be interpreted to good effect. The almond green of the door is lifted and complemented by the contrasting warm pink of the woven willow-cane chairs. The billowing, floor-to-ceiling cream curtains add a note of softness and create a sense of depth and space.

YELLOW-GREEN

In its clearest form, yellow-green is evocative of new leaf growth and is a useful decorating colour with which to bring a touch of advancing brightness to a scheme without the heat or stridence of bright reds or oranges. In more muted or dulled tones, the colour is less intense and demanding.

Yellow-green creates a striking resonance incorporated in small amounts among other colours such as blues, purples or reds. Used alongside white, it appears clean, cool and fresh. It works well in larger quantities if punctuated by pictures, ornaments and decorative objects.

There is no yellow-green pigment although there are numerous vegetable dyes which produce the colour. In paint form, however, it is best mixed from lemon yellow and either a blue-green such as a viridian, or even a greenish blue like cerulean. It can also be made by adding black to lemon yellow; this produces a less intense colour.

Yellow-green can be lightened with white. When mixed with umber, a less clear, more muted, duller version of the colour is produced.

Above The subdued yellow-green of this primitive painting in a house near Grasse, in France, might be lost in a busier setting. Here, its subtlety is enhanced by the white walls, grey shelves and natural stone of the mantel.

Right This English bedroom uses colour sparingly to give a delicate, spring-like atmosphere. The brightest colour is the yellow-green of the chair cushions, curtain bows and the small-print pattern of the wallpaper. The green is strong but not saturated, and therefore not overpowering. The eighteenth-century painted chair introduces a small amount of deep golden ochre and the embroidered pictures add touches of mid-toned earthy reds and greens. The ebonized furniture adds weight to the design, while the off-white curtains, woodwork and wallpaper lighten the room. *Designer: Merlin Pennink*

Far right Compared with the green of the bedroom, the green of these library walls is somewhat muted, as are the reds, blues and yellows of the painted bookcase, and the bindings of the books. The equality of tone between the colours produces a surprisingly harmonious and restful effect. The bookcase – now at Charleston – was handpainted by Duncan Grant in about 1925 for Clive Bell.

Right The principal colour in this room is an intense lime green, glazed and distressed. A paler version of it is used on the chairs and deeper, more muted shades in the other fabrics. The second colour used is the complementary. The bright pink in the curtains, the maroon cushion and deep lacquer-red Chinese cabinet give the room a lively character.

The furniture needs to make a positive statement in the company of these strong colours. This makes the black table, stools and cabinet a good choice. Some areas of neutral colour – the polished wood floor and the curtain ground – prevent a rich scheme becoming overwhelming.

To reproduce the wall colour shown here, use yellow-green as the undercoat and then rag on a little darker green glaze. *Designer: Georgina Fairholme*

Left This collection of nineteenth-century vaseline glass catches the light and creates a lustrous pool of yellow-greens. The effect is enhanced by the subtle arrangement of yellow-green flowers: fennel, euphorbia and lady's mantle (*Alchemilla mollis*).

Right The dining room of this converted cottage mixes intense and muted yellow-greens with terracotta to good effect. The first wall you see when you open the front door is painted in a strong yellow-green. An off-white wall separates it from a wall painted a dark olive. Grey-green skirting adds a lighter note. The brownish red of the quarry tiles and hall table acts as the complementary, and the carpet combines both colours with dark blue.

OLIVE GREEN

Olive green is the colour of an olive on its tree. It is a dark, dense, drab colour – a muted shade of cool yellow or yellow-green.

Olive is a colour often associated with house painting in the eighteenth century and in the early years of the nineteenth. The neo-classical fashion for imitating patinated bronze by dusting bronze powder over drab green paint also accounted for the colour's popularity. In the late nineteenth century it was combined with aesthetic shades of yellow, blue and red.

As a dull earthy colour, olive looks good with its complementary, scarlet, and with the brighter earth colours such as Venetian red, Indian red and light red. It harmonizes with light cool yellows and gold seems to bring it to life.

Above The Arts and Crafts pottery designer William de Morgan achieved a rich variety of olive greens in these wall tiles. The pigment used was copper oxide; its true colour only becomes apparent after firing.

Right The walls of the drawing room at Wightwick Manor, near Wolverhampton, are hung with woven silk and wool fabric in the 'Dove and Rose' pattern designed by William Morris in 1879. The Wightwick version is in the colours described by Gilbert and Sullivan in *Patience* as 'greenery-yallery'.

Morris's interest in traditional craftsmanship led him to use only natural dyes, such as woad, indigo, weld and madder, with harmonious results.

Far right The walls and ceiling of this study in a house in Basle, Switzerland, have been lined with a soft-textured olive green fabric as a backdrop for a collection of antiques and pictures. Small touches of complementary red give life to the dulled green.

Above The play of light, pattern, contour and texture – duplicated in the ornate full-length mirror – gives an almost sculptural quality to this white landing. One of the most simple of colours, white can be used to bring the elegance of different materials and forms into focus: here, plain white walls and glossed banisters meet the rich gilt of the mirror and the more muted and golden hues of the natural wooden floor and stairwell, showing the latter off to fine advantage.

Right above A four-poster bed, swathed romantically in white material, provides a dramatic focus for this room. The honey tones of the Andalusian floor tiles and the dark wooden furniture and doors make a pleasing contrast to the white colour scheme. The result is fresh yet restful. Through the open doors is a view of the rolling hills of southern Spain; inside, the bed is cool and inviting.

Right below The simplicity of white can be used to delicate and romantic effect. Warm, off-white walls and a natural wood floor give a soft glow to this arrangement. The textured pattern of the embroidered tablecloth and the neat ticking chair covers add depth and interest. A gentle light filters in through the curtains, moulding the objects it falls on with highlights and shadows and accentuating the sheen of the polished floor.

WHITE

In its purest form, white is the colour of snow, chalk and lilies. It has been used in many regions for hundreds of years – in the form of limewash and distemper, for example – to decorate both the exterior and interior of buildings. White lead pigment was used by the Romans and Chinese from very early times but most people based their decorating whites on chalk or lime.

White was a popular decorating colour for walls and ceilings in the second half of the eighteenth century, often offset by gilding or used as a foil for stronger colours. It was not a bright white and had a tendency to yellow and darken with age. Plain and patterned white fabrics were also used – white bedlinen and bedcovers enjoying a particular vogue. Unlike the chemically bleached materials

of today, these fabrics were sometimes laid out in the sun to whiten.

The white rooms and furniture designed by Charles Rennie Mackintosh in the early years of the twentieth century marked a significant departure from the flamboyant, rich and sombre colours used in the nineteenth century. But it was not until the 1920s – following the introduction in 1919 of titanium oxide, a brighter, more stable white – that the colour became highly fashionable and its use more widespread. In the twenties and thirties, white schemes were variously interpreted by leading design figures such as Basil Ionides, Syrie Maugham and Elsie de Wolfe. More recently, interior decorators such as John Fowler have used subtly modulated shades of 'dirty white' on different surfaces and mouldings to help accentuate textural variation and to achieve a sense of contrast and depth.

Decorating whites vary greatly in both texture and tone – whether in paintwork, fabric, floorcovering or chinaware – and can be combined to create a vast range of different moods.

Above The brightness of this room on Long Island is relieved by the introduction of contrast and texture. White predominates but is brought to life by the rough cream-coloured rug and smooth limed floor. These neutral colours make a fine background for the dark wood furniture, black fireplace and wall-mounted antique clock. The arrangement of lamps, candlesticks and pictures adds symmetry and precision.

Right Light is all-important in this photographic studio in a converted warehouse in Melbourne, Australia: it is allowed to penetrate everywhere – via the skylights and large Japanese-style sliding doors – reflecting off the glossy white ceramic floor tiles to increase the feeling of size and sense of spacious elegance. Furnishings are kept to minimum. Two simple marble-topped columns, displaying statues of Balinese dancers, flank the doorway and are juxtaposed with an elegant antique chair; the windows and doors are hung with warmer, off-white curtains to give some softness and contrast in texture. The sliding doors open out on to the cool aquamarine tones of a painted courtyard. In this way, both focus and colour are skilfully introduced into the interior.

CREAM

Cream is one of the most versatile colours in decoration and can work well with many styles of interior, from the classical and grand to the modest and simple.

The colour was popular throughout the eighteenth century, sometimes offset by gilded details. It was used in paintwork – for example, on columns or alcoves – on chair covers or moiré wall panels. Cream interiors, in which furnishings and fabrics were as important as paintwork, were also a feature of the design schemes of the 1930s. Much Art Deco work used cream

Above In the late-seventeenth-century drawing room of Huntingdon Castle, southern Ireland, the colour cream has been used to enhance the sense of antiquity. The formal symmetry of the mantelpiece and the arrangement of smooth glazed chinaware stand out against the rough, cream-coloured plaster walls – as here, contrasts in texture, surface and form can provide an appealing focus for a room. Touches of red and green on the plates provide a lively contrast to the interplay of wood, gilt and cream.

Right White-on-white colour schemes can achieve bold and sophisticated effects. Shades of cream and white are used on the walls and furnishings of an Empire-style drawing room. The contrasting dark tones of the pictures and the lacquered wood stand out boldly against these neutral colours, giving the room strength and definition. *Designer: Raymond Liberatori*

Far right The simple lines of this modern room are given a classic elegance through the use of creams, neutrals and a starkly contrasting area of black. The pale tones of the sofa, shelves and wall are modulated by the bleached wooden floor and the colour-washed grey wall behind the dark fireplace. *Designers: Hariri and Hariri*

alongside touches of more dominant colours such as turquoise, mauve, orange or lime green.

As a warm, neutral colour, cream combines successfully with most other colours apart from the highly saturated primaries which can overwhelm its subtle earthiness. It is particularly effective alongside colours of a strong contrast such as black, deep green or dark blue; gold or gilt detailing with cream gives a classical, romantic and elegant atmosphere. Cream is often used as a main colour in a room or as a soothing link between stronger colours and can be mixed from white with a touch of yellow ochre or Naples yellow.

Above The mellow, weathered hues of this neo-classical stone frieze encapsulate the timeless elegance of cream.

Left A subtle harmony of texture, colour and light has been achieved in this room, using natural materials in several shades of cream. A touch of ochre, mixed with white, gives the wall its creamy warmth. Light filters in through the bamboo blinds and catches the glaze of the pots. *Designer: John Stefanidis*

Far left A light, romantic mood has been created here, using a dark charcoal colour on a cream background, a far cry from the harsh, sombre effects often associated with dark colours. The intricate damask design of the wallpaper is reminiscent of Spanish lace or Elizabethan blackwork embroidery. The rich cream and the soft, warm black work well with the brown of the wooden chair and floor and the Moorish-style star-shaped brass light. *Designer: Miranda Humphries*

133

BROWN

Brown has a wide range of shades – the deep or muted hues of yellow, orange, red and violet produce a wonderful selection of different colours.

In the mid seventeenth century, varying shades of brown were introduced into interiors through elaborate wood panelling and carving. The strong, dark hues of the early eighteenth century included deep brown paintwork – used frequently on doors – and brown printed fabrics. Often combined with gold, buff or mauve, the colour also played a significant role in Victorian Britain when rich, heavy interiors and furnishings were fashionable.

The ability of brown to demonstrate warmth as well as coolness means that it can be used as a foil for strong, exotic or vibrant colours, such as shocking pink or bright turquoise, which may otherwise be difficult to match. Use it to tone down strong reds, blues or greens; place it with creamy white for a warm, inviting effect.

Browns can be mixed from umber pigments: raw umber produces a cool, slightly greenish colour while burnt umber gives a warmer chocolate colour.

Above These snuff boxes in the shape of shoes, some dating from as early as 1730, are fashioned out of a variety of woods – from yellow satinwood to rich, polished mahogany and ebony. The collection displays a range of warm browns, offset by the surrounding reds, greens and yellows.

Right Spicy colours have been used to create elegance and cosiness in this interior. The English eighteenth-century campaign bed is canopied in a striped, warm sienna brown silk, lined with yellow and covered with a patterned nineteenth-century brown chintz quilt. The colours in the French floral wallpaper are picked up in the grey-green paintwork and yellow lampshades of the adjoining room. *Designer: David Mlinaric*

Far right Here is a perfect example of the rustic simplicity that can be achieved using a range of browns in different materials and textures. Dark woods, scrubbed pine and rush-matting work harmoniously with mid-brown and creamy yellow paintwork. The mahogany brown picture rail holds the colour scheme together.

Left The dining room of a Siamese teak house shows how dark, rich brown woods can be combined to create an effect that works in any interior. While the darkness is cool and soothing, the warmth of the polished wood predominates. The richness of the wood is contrasted with delicate blue-and-white Ming china.

Below left This bedroom is part of an eighteenth-century Dutch-style barn that was transported from its original location in New Jersey to a new site in East Hampton. When reconstructed, the oak was turned inside out so that the patina of the last two centuries would appear on the inside of the building. And the varying brown tones of the old wooden walls are a fine example of how restful and natural the colour of wood

can be. *Architects: Gwathmey, Siegel and Associates. Interior designer: Courtney Sale Ross*

Right These painted shelves are surrounded by brown and black prints, embellished with a touch of pink. The lattice work of the china is echoed in the colour and design of the delicate wallpaper. This is a fine example of a simple and elegant dry brown.

Below right Wallpaper in shades of soft apricot gives added warmth to the orange-brown of an antique quilt. Floor-to-ceiling chintz curtains echo the apricot and brown and also pick up the blue of the Victorian nursing chair. The crisp white of the embroidered sheets and the touches of blue counterbalance the warmer browns and apricots. *Designer: Diana Griffin-Strauss*

NEUTRALS

Dark and light neutrals are mixed, muddied shades, many of which are derived from greys and browns – for example, taupe, fawn, drab, beige and stone. Others, including biscuit, sand, camel and buff have a slight yellow tinge, while colours such as mushroom and khaki are more complex mixtures.

Stone, a neutral colour, was used widely in the Palladian period and was mixed from lead white and sienna or umber pigments. Alongside pea green, it was the main decorating colour of the eighteenth century. After being ground in nut oil, the colour was applied in layers to woodwork and walls. Drab, a dull light brown or yellowish brown, also features prominently in decorating history. An 1876 edition of *Queen* magazine – outlining an ideal interior

Above The ornate detailing in this impressive Gothic room has been picked out in white to give freshness to a gentle wall colour of mushroom. Blue-and-white china, richly-coloured leather-bound books and an arrangement of framed silhouettes lend sparkle to the room's subtle, dark neutral tones.

Right Natural, neutral colours combined in subtle tones are soothing and mellow. Here, a tapestry landscape provides the backdrop for the brown-grey hues of a limed oak sideboard displaying an assortment of fir cones and dried flowers and grasses. *Designer: Annie Sloan*

Far right Light, spaciousness and simplicity are the keynotes of this interior, the guest bedroom of a house in Nantucket, off Cape Cod. The creamy white emulsioned (latexed) walls and limed oak floor are offset by the greeny grey paintwork of the skirting, window frames, sills and wainscot. The owner scraped back and burnt off the original paintwork, then sanded the wood which, with traces of the paint-colour left in it, revealed a dark neutral green-grey colour.

colour scheme of the time – offers a useful point of reference:

'Hall and staircase: sober yellowish drab and high red dado with two lines of white.

Dining room: walls dark drab, with high dado of mauve and drab in alternate colours.'

John Fowler and Nancy Lancaster used a range of neutrals – including drab, taupe and khaki – to lend depth and elegance to their designs.

These gentle, muted hues combine well with natural textures and surfaces. Unpolished wood, limed oak, bleached pine, coir matting, hessian – all can form the basis of a neutral colour scheme.

Neutrals work well with each other as well as with single colour or multi colour schemes. They are often used to separate or reduce the impact of two or more other colours and can provide both punctuation and change of pace in a room. Interiors designed exclusively from neutral colours are relaxing, calm and undemanding.

Left The cool, pale colours used in this bedroom enhance the effect of the light streaming in through the window. Elaborate, full curtains of a dramatic dark blue damask and a rich, eighteenth-century bedspread add depth and detail. The coir matting on the floor and the light neutral walls, with their slightly green tinge, give a feeling of spaciousness to the room. *Decorator: Keith Day*

Above Beautifully painted *trompe l'oeil* swagged material and stonework cover the walls of this distinctive bathroom. The comparative warmth of the 'material' is offset by the deliberate cold, stone effect. The room itself was painted with artist's oil colour in

two tones of buff, mixed with glaze and given a coat of polyurethane. The colours in the room show a light, delicate range of greys, sands and beiges. *Decorator: Keith Day*

Right The textural contrast of walls, flooring and upholstery in this room gives life to the pale colours used. *Trompe l'oeil* stone walls and a marble-topped table are countered by the more informal arrangement of armchairs and side tables. The neutral tones and the symmetry of the room's design give a classical appearance. Splashes of contrasting colour in the richly textured armchair and footstool add an essential touch of warmth to the room's stark sophistication. *Designer: Mark Hampton*

GREY

The vast range of different greys extend from the warmer brownish, greenish or pinkish tones – often quite complex combinations – through to the cooler colours that tend to be based on either blue or simple black-and-white mixtures.

With the concern for a return to the simplicity and harmony of classical design, grey mouldings were used in Renaissance interiors to offset plain white plaster walls. In the early eighteenth century, grey was among the limited range of paints available.

The texture and finish chosen for greys is all-important: they tend to work well in glaze or silk paint. Grey can be a cool, sophisticated colour but, equally – particularly when pinky greys are used – can be made to look peaceful, soft, warm and soothing. It works well with most other colours including pink, pale blue, bright green and vermilion.

Left Exquisitely rich colours work together powerfully with green-greys in this sumptuous yet intimate library-study. The deep orange-red lacquered walls and the rich warm reds and browns in the woods and carpets are offset by the grey of the doors and ceiling. To give depth and interest, three tones of green-grey have been used – dark and mid-tones on the door panels and the lightest of all on the ceiling. A display of blue-and-white china lends freshness to the scheme. *Designer: David Mlinaric*

Above This room makes use of a subtle range of modulated green-greys: the paint on the Queen Anne panelling is an artist's oil colour mixed with glaze; a lighter tone is used for the ceiling and an even paler tone for the cornice. The dark frames of the botanical prints stand out smartly against the grey, while the dark fireplace, seventeenth-century chandelier, Chippendale chairs and wood floor contribute to the contrasting colour scheme and give solidity and definition. The Aubusson carpet and rose pink damask blinds bring a welcome warmth to the room. *Decorator: Keith Day*

Right A pale grey glaze mixture was applied on to the walls of this bathroom to give a clean, fresh look. A delicate stencilled border echoes the antique Greek lace at the window. The dark stained oak bath surround and frame give the room strength and depth.

Above James McNeill Whistler's *Miss Cicely Alexander: Harmony in Grey and Green* encapsulates the soft delicacy and subtlety of effect that can be achieved using a range of cool greys in varying tones and textures.

Below Here, the wrought iron of the staircase is painted a cool grey and its distinctive pattern is silhouetted against the softly-lit, undulating colours of the wall. The delicate pink of the wall above and the marbled pink and cream below, provide a soft, warm backdrop for the grey. This elegant stairway is in a classical period house – the colours used are suitably refined and tranquil.

Right A range of blue-greys was used to create the painted *trompe l'oeil* curtain that decorates this unusual bedroom. Despite the apparent coolness of the greys, the swathes of hanging fabric have an implied warmth. With the neutral tones of the overall colour scheme – white bedlinen, silver, pine, ceramics and grey flooring – the result is a peaceful room in which no one colour predominates. *Artist: Michael Falkard*

BLACK & WHITE

The combination of black and white is an old yet simple and striking decorating device. While black is dark and receding, white is light and advancing – the colours work powerfully together because they are complete opposites and thus provide maximum visual contrast.

The two colours can be put together in many different ways but are particularly eyecatching used in geometric form – as wall or floor tiles, for example – in an overall pattern reminiscent of Elizabethan blackwork embroidery or in minimalist interiors using modern objects and materials.

Black and white can work effectively alongside other colours in design schemes although these are often best used sparingly so as not to detract from the dramatic impact. Clear colours work best, especially strong, intense colours such as scarlet or gold.

Above Black-and-white floor tiles have a long history in European interior design schemes. This painting by Gonzales Coques, depicting an early seventeenth-century Dutch interior, shows black and white set against the rich colours of tapestry-woven textile furnishings and golden Netherlandish wood panelling. As illustrated here, black and white combines well with brass detailing.

Right A similar distinctive combination of wood with black-and-white flooring is used in the entrance hall of this house in Thailand. The rich, warm tones of the wood, with its slightly reddish hues and glossy sheen, offset the black-and-white Italian marble floor to create a space which is at once warm and welcoming.

The unambiguous, dramatic effect of black with white lends itself to geometric design. In the sitting area of a house on Long Island (**left**), small areas and strong lines of black give balance, proportion and delineation against a predominance of white. Touches of ochre, gilt and brass add detail and texture.

The same colours, used to quite different effect, have been combined in a kitchen (**below right**) in which a large black range takes centre stage. White and neutral tones help to maximize the effect of light while warmth is introduced in touches of copper, earthenware, wood and in the stove's brass fittings.

A more stringent opposition of the two colours has been achieved in this stylish bathroom (**below left**), with its black carpet and arrangement of black tiles against white. Reminiscent of Art Deco style, the design is refreshingly direct and simple.

Left A variation of the black-and-white theme is shown in this view of the late eighteenth-century dining room of a château near Le Mans. Whites, combined in various textures, shades and materials are offset by just a touch of black. An antique Dutch porcelain stove is juxtaposed with the softer lines of the white throw-over sheeting and a gentle wall colour of cream. The dark detailing on the stove is played off against the black diamond floor tiles: both give strength and definition to the colour scheme.

Right The long, narrow hallway of a former gunpowder factory, built in 1793, lent itself to dramatic decorative treatment. A strong emphasis on the contrast of black and white accentuates the hall's angular lines: the white walls, ceiling and woodwork offset the granite-topped console with its silver plate and collection of black marble spheres. A pale creamy beige carpet provides some variation to the black-and-white theme. Overhead recessed halogen lights cast strong shadows, while tungsten uplighters, housed in narrow columns either side of the hallway, give a softer, more general light. Black-framed mirrors help to give an illusion of space. With lithographs by contemporary artists lining the walls, the overall effect is that of a picture gallery. *Designer: Mary Fox Linton*

BLACK

There are many degrees and tones of black: soft grey-blacks, brown and reddish blacks, cool blue-blacks. Names such as anthracite, ebony and jet black designate the deepest tones.

Until the twentieth century, black was most often incorporated in design schemes through decorative detailing or fabrics. In the 1920s in England, it was very much in vogue and was used not only as a background colour for fabrics such as chintzes and damasks but also, more daringly, for walls and ceilings.

Its absorption of all light makes black a highly textural colour – a matt black surface is dense while a glossy black surface reflects more light and is vibrant and positive. Black makes other colours come alive and used in detailing, it can add vigour and definition to a room.

Left The jet black floor and fittings in this kitchen create a sense of functionalism and cleanliness. The room's strongly geometric lines – apparent in the mesh ceiling and wall covering, the Venetian blinds, black track light fittings and tiled floor – help to diffuse the flat, dense effect that black can sometimes have. The pale golden hues of the wooden door, shelves and detailing offset the black and give definition to the room.

Far left Black is a strong wall colour for a room of this size, but skilful use of space and decoration creates a luxurious and intimate atmosphere. Reflective and gloss surfaces maximize the effect of light while the black lacquer-effect walls provide a dramatic foil for the white, yellow, gilt and gold detailing. Ceiling lamps ensure that light bounces off as many surfaces as possible; a large mirror reflects the light filtering through the shutters and adds depth and dimension to the bathroom. Texture and pattern are introduced through the checkered, stained pine floor, pine window shutters and detailing on fabrics and material. *Designer: Anoushka Hempel*

Overleaf The black walls of Charleston's dining room allow the colours in ceramics, pictures and furnishings to stand out boldly. Earthy matt reds, greens and ochres and areas of neutral colour – including a whitewashed ceiling and a coconut-matting floor – prevent the black from being overwhelming and give the room a rustic, informal atmosphere. The greenish grey of the circular table – painted by Vanessa Bell in the 1950s – with its black-and-white border, provides a link with the walls and the painted grey door.

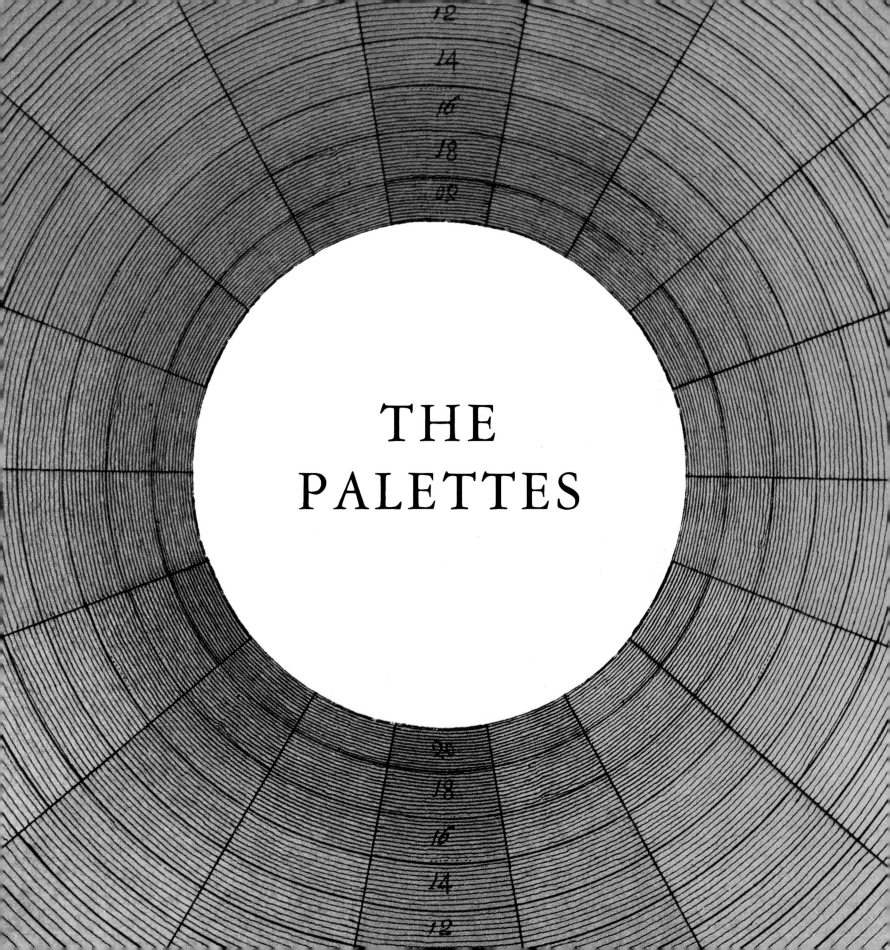

THE
PALETTES

EARTH COLOURS

These colours, derived from naturally occurring pigments, belong in the same tonal range and harmonize well together. They tend to be browns tinged, perhaps, with hints of red, yellow or green. Blues, purples and bright greens are more rare, but white and black are provided by chalk or lime and soot or charcoal and are in plentiful supply.

This basic palette has been available to almost every culture in the world. The colours have been used in all forms of decoration from cottage walls and tempera paintings to primitive pots and tribal war-paint.

In an age before mass-production, each community would rely on the colours available locally. These regional associations still persist in the pigment names: Oxford ochre, Venetian pink, burnt sienna.

Although some of the earth colours can be quite bright, they are never crude. In decoration, they are often used either against or mixed in with large quantities of white. In parts of France an earth pigment is added directly to the wall plaster, making it unnecessary to paint the wall. Elsewhere, pigments are mixed with any whitish medium to create a subtly coloured tint. In East Anglia, for example, red is added to the whitewash to give houses a distinctive pink colour.

Below left A painted wall decoration in Orissa State, India (courtesy of Barbara Lloyd); below right The frescoed anteroom of the early 16th-century Villa Querini, near Venice

Opposite page: above Aboriginal artefacts in an 1850s Australian homestead; below left The rooftops of wooden houses by a Norwegian fjord; below right The conservatory of a house in the Cotswolds, England

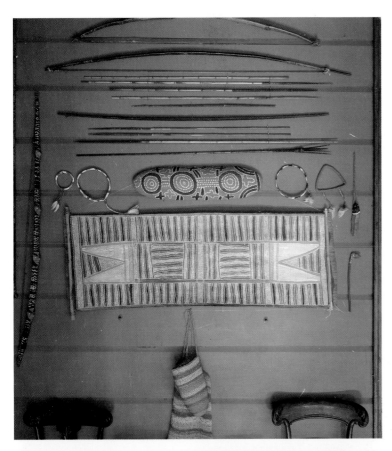

RARE COLOURS

Rare and expensive colours that are more intense and lustrous than common earth pigments have always enjoyed a special regard. They tend to be derived from pure minerals such as lapis lazuli, malachite, realgar, orpiment, vermilion and azurite. In places where these rare minerals were – and are – unavailable other, brighter colours were often exploited. The Aztecs of Mexico, for example, extracted a bright red dye from the dried bodies of the cochineal insect.

In their pure forms such colours were too expensive to find much place in domestic decoration except, perhaps, in minute quantities. In the eighteenth and nineteenth centuries, however, the advancement in chemical methods permitted intense colours to be produced more cheaply. Gradually, the old mineral colours were superseded by more readily available substitutes: lapis lazuli by ultramarine, malachite by viridian, orpiment and realgar by cadmium yellow, and vermilion and cinnabar by cadmium red. Although the historic originals of these colours were not found in domestic interiors, ceramics and other works of art provide a source of inspiration for using their modern equivalents in decoration today.

Left Titian's *Bacchus and Ariadne,* 1522–3;
below left A late 16th-century Turkish dish;
below right *Portrait of Babur* Mughal India,
c. 1610

Opposite page: above Duccio's *The Virgin
and Child,* c. 1300; **below** The dining room
of the 18th-century Bantry House, County
Cork, southern Ireland

TRADITIONAL COLOURS

In Britain, Europe and North America throughout much of the eighteenth century, a limited range of muted, drab and earth colours, sometimes enlivened with gold decoration, was used on walls, ceilings, woodwork and furniture. Greens and browns were prevalent and a dulled mid green (known also as Georgian green) was particularly popular for panelled rooms throughout northern Europe.

These colours were often harmonized with neutral hues of similar tone – drabs, greys, putty colours and off-whites mixed from umber.

Above left A bedchamber and anteroom in Skogaholm Manor, Stockholm; above right Room in an 18th-century Scottish house; right The attic of a restored early 19th-century Federal-style house in North Carolina

Opposite page: above left Boucher's *La Modiste*, painted in the late 1740s; right Arthur Devis's *The Duet*, 1749, a 'conversation piece'

THE ROCOCO

By the early eighteenth century in Europe, the robust grandeur of Baroque had begun to give way to a style which, while equally ornate, was lighter and more fanciful in colour and design. The paintings of Boucher and Watteau epitomized the colours and atmosphere of the new style, known as Rococo.

During this period, the decorator's palette was characterized by light tones and subtle pastels. The personal taste of Madame de Pompadour, mistress of Louis XV, was highly influential in interior decoration. She revitalized the Aubusson tapestry factory and founded the porcelain works at Sèvres and demanded new patterns and colours from these sources. Powder Pink, Apple Green, French Lilac, Pompadour Blue, Oriental Gold, Sèvres Blue, Rose Pompadour, Palace Cream and Cloud White – the very names of the colours denote airiness and elegance.

Opposite page: **above left** Sir William Chambers RA (attrib.), 'Design for Throne with Baldacchino' c. 1782; **right** The hall of 18th-century Lebell Manor, Finland

Below Design for an 18th-century Beauvais tapestry (after Boucher); **above right** Modern room using wallpaper and fabric based on an 18th-century Reveillon design; **below right** Sitting room of a London house

BRIGHT COLOURS

Towards the end of the eighteenth century and at the beginning of the nineteenth there was a great revival of interest in the architecture and decoration of ancient Greece and Rome. Designers such as Robert Adam in Britain combined the strong, brilliant and arresting colours they had seen in Italy – reds, lilacs, terracottas, clean blues and greens – in their own innovative interior schemes.

Napoleon's taste for a Classical revival favoured even more pronounced colours and marked a departure from the subtle shades of the Rococo. The creation of very bright colours with synthetic chemical sources expanded this palette considerably. The Empire style used bright, deep greens, purples, lemon yellows and ruby reds against white grounds and gold motifs.

Left Empire-style drawing room; **below left**
Design for the drawing room ceiling at Syon
House by Robert Adam, 1762, watercolour;
below Design for a printed cotton, French,
c. 1810–15

Opposite page: above View of the hallway
from a reception room at the early
nineteenth-century Homewood House,
Baltimore; **below** Illustration from Theodore
Pasquier's *Dessins d'ameublement*, Paris,
c. 1830

VICTORIAN COLOURS

The Victorians had more colours available to them than their predecessors. The discovery of synthetic, or aniline, dyes in 1856 produced a range of purples and brilliant pinks. Also of significance in this period was the introduction of alizarin crimson, viridian, cerulean blue and the willowy green chromium oxide.

The Victorians combined a large number of colours and strong patterns to create polychromatic schemes. Colours were rarely used in their most intense form. Contrary to the airy brightness of much Regency decoration, more sombre shades were preferred: rich greens, slate greys and bright reds muddied with brown or made purple with blue.

BALLET RUSSE & ART DECO

In the early twentieth century, designers began to use a large range of intense and vivid colours in new ways. Diaghilev's Ballet Russe arrived in Paris in 1909 and introduced to Western Europe a rich legacy of Russian decorative art. Leon Bakst's flamboyant designs incorporated brilliant emerald and lime greens, lilacs, purples and bright oranges. These were juxtaposed with black and midnight blue to accentuate their brilliance and jewel-like quality. Gold and silver were also used.

Art Deco, first seen at the 1925 Paris Exhibition, was slightly more angular and less flamboyant in style than Bakst's designs. The principal colours were orange and green – the latter varied from greyish celadon to bluish minty colours.

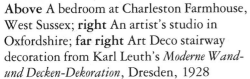

Above A bedroom at Charleston Farmhouse, West Sussex; **right** An artist's studio in Oxfordshire; **far right** Art Deco stairway decoration from Karl Leuth's *Moderne Wand- und Decken-Dekoration*, Dresden, 1928

Opposite page: above Dinner service designed by Dame Laura Knight in the 1930s; **below** 'Modern Bedroom in Vivid Colouring', illustration from Edward Thorne's *Decorative Draperies and Upholstery*, 1929

TROPICAL COLOURS

Decoration in a tropical climate often demands strong, bright colours that can stand up to glaring sun and deep shade.

The range of tropical colours is wide – even chaotic – but the jumble of reds, blues, greens and yellows tends to share a common clarity and brightness that gives them a certain harmony. And the harshness of the tropical light often blurs the distinctness of the hues, allowing colour schemes which combine, say, a bright turquoise with a warm ultramarine, or scarlet and a crimson.

Although tropical colours are mostly clear, they do not have the blatant simplicity of unadulterated primaries and secondaries. Often, a touch of a second colour gives them added character.

Above *Englishman on an Elephant, Shooting at a Tiger*, c. 1830, watercolour; **left** The temple courtyard, Jodhpur (courtesy of Barbara Lloyd)

Opposite page: above Arrangement of tropical fruit in a dining room in Mexico City; **below** Tree-top-high deck of a house in Echo Park, Los Angeles

THE MODERN PALETTE

The work of the Bauhaus school of architecture and applied arts was one of the key influences upon the development of the 'modern' palette. Established in Germany in 1919 by Walter Gropius, the Bauhaus sought to apply the principles of function and form to all areas of design.

In its colour schemes, the Bauhaus advocated the clear and the arrestingly simple. The recent discovery of titanium dioxide had made good-quality white paint readily available and it was used extensively. Against this white background the modernists would also set areas of strong colour, often making use of primary colours and black.

Above A reproduction of Gerrit Rietveld's *Red-Blue* chair, c. 1917–18; **above right** *Autumn Leaves*, Aubusson tapestry, 1971; **right** Modern London sitting room

PAINT
& COLOUR
MIXING

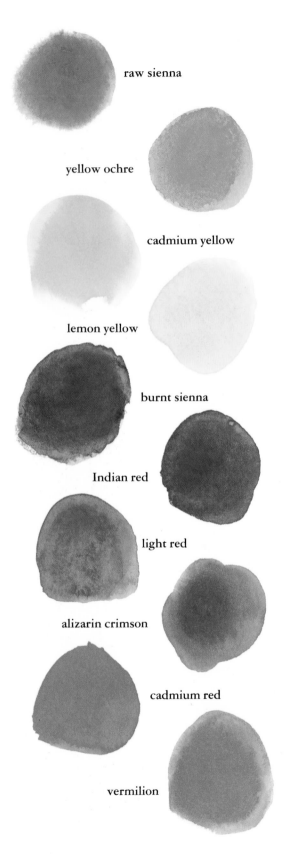

raw sienna

yellow ochre

cadmium yellow

lemon yellow

burnt sienna

Indian red

light red

alizarin crimson

cadmium red

vermilion

PIGMENTS

Paint contains two main ingredients: the source of colour – or pigment – and the medium that carries that colour. The pigments we buy for decorating usually come suspended in oil, as artist's or student's oil colours, or acrylic in powdered form or as universal stainers. They are created from a variety of organic and inorganic sources and there are synthetic, inexpensive renderings of both.

Readers interested in establishing the historical authenticity of colours used in interior decoration should bear in mind that in the nineteenth century there was commonly an interval of about twenty years between the invention of a pigment and its commercial availability.

The development of synthetic colours in the last hundred years has provided more choice for the decorator, but most effects can be obtained from a relatively few pigments. Illustrated here are those we most often use. But before looking at these individual pigments their general qualities need explanation.

Pigments vary in their capacity for covering a surface. Opaque colours, such as cadmium red and cerulean blue, cover previous colour effectively. The more transparent pigments are influenced by underlying colours and can, for example, be applied over

Raw sienna comes from clay containing iron and manganese. The best quality is found in Italy near Siena. Redder and browner than yellow ochre, it is less opaque but reliably permanent.

Yellow ochre also comes from natural clay coloured by iron, found in many parts of the world. Available in a variety of dull yellow shades, it is opaque and permanent.

Cadmium yellow, from cadmium sulphide, replaces the earlier, less permanent chrome yellows. It comes in a range of warm shades, all of brilliant intensity and semi-transparent.

Lemon yellow is a cooler, paler transparent yellow. The best varieties are based on arylide, cadmium and barium.

Burnt sienna is made by roasting raw sienna in a furnace. A rich, brilliant colour, it is permanent and transparent but low in tinting strength. It is the least chalky of the red browns and adds a useful depth and clarity to mixtures.

Indian red, a bluish, opaque, permanent pigment which replaces Spanish red, has

good tinting strength and can be mixed with white or used as a wash to obtain rosy pinks.

Light red, which replaces Venetian red, describes the more intense Mars or English red pure oxides which are brighter and more scarlet in tone than Indian red. Light red is opaque, has good tinting strength and, when mixed with white or used as a wash, makes a variety of salmon pinks.

Alizarin crimson is a synthetic organic pigment, first introduced in 1868. A cool red, it has replaced the Madder reds and carmine lakes. Clear and transparent, it is a good glazing pigment.

Cadmium red, available since the 1920s, is composed of three parts cadmium sulphide and two parts cadmium selenide, it is a warm red leaning towards orange. Opaque and durable, it has good covering quality and adequate tinting strength.

Vermilion, mercuric sulphide, was first used in Europe in the eighteenth century. It is a very opaque bright red, but its permanence is not reliable – some grades have a tendency to turn black.

white to create subtle tints. Intense pigments, such as French ultramarine and Prussian blue, cover well because of their depth of colour even though they are transparent.

Some pigments have a high tinting strength – a little has a powerful effect – while others, such as cobalt blue and chromium green oxide, are much weaker.

All the pigments shown should be sufficiently permanent for normal use. The earth colours – ochres, siennas and umbers – and the cobalt and cerulean blues are absolutely permanent. The quality, too, of the earth colours is good and even cheaper versions of these pigments are reliable. Others such as cadmium red, alizarin crimson and cerulean and cobalt blue are more variable and lower-grades should be avoided.

The effect of a pigment may vary according to the medium it is carried in. Once dry, gloss paint, for example, appears lighter than an emulsion of the same colour. Pigments also differ according to make; ask for advice, particularly when choosing colours known to be variable – earth colours, such as raw umber and light red, and the high grades of French ultramarine, cadmium red and phthalocyanine green.

Bear in mind that some pigments have undertones which differ from their top tones. Such undertones become more evident when using a thin coat of a transparent colour, as in a glaze, or when diluting an opaque pigment with white.

Raw umber comes from natural clay which contains more manganese than that used for raw sienna. The tones of this cool dark brown vary from greenish to violet-brown and it is semi-opaque; an absolutely permanent pigment.

Burnt umber, made by roasting raw umber, is warmer, redder and more transparent than the raw pigment. Permanent, with good tinting strength, it can be mixed with ultramarine to produce deep powerful shades or blacks.

French ultramarine was originally made by grinding lapis lazuli but has been produced artificially since 1828. A warmish blue, tending to violet, it is an extremely intense colour with high tinting strength and covering power, although semi-transparent; it is permanent in most uses.

Prussian blue, ferric-ferrocyanide, was introduced as a pigment in about 1724. It is an intense greenish blue, but since it is not always permanent, it is often replaced by the permanent phthalocyanine blue which has the same properties and appearance. Both blues are transparent but of very high tinting strength.

Cobalt blue, a compound of cobalt oxide, aluminium oxide and phosphoric acid, is a permanent, bright colour. Similar to ultramarine but not so deep or intense, it has an underlying greenish hue.

Cerulean blue, made from a compound of tin oxides and cobalt, is an expensive pigment. A strong light blue with a greenish tone, it is opaque and reliably permanent.

Terre verte, green earth, is a natural pigment containing iron and manganese. Semi-transparent in oil with low tinting and covering power, it has more body in a water-based medium.

Chromium oxide green, known since 1809, is a pale, cool opaque pigment. Its tinting power is not strong but it is entirely permanent for all uses.

Phthalocyanine green, introduced in 1938, is a permanent transparent pigment with very high tinting power.

Lamp black is made from pure carbon and is a cool bluish black. It is permanent and has good covering and tinting power.

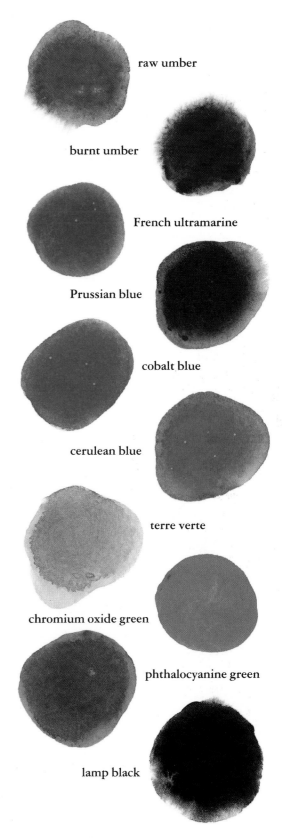

raw umber

burnt umber

French ultramarine

Prussian blue

cobalt blue

cerulean blue

terre verte

chromium oxide green

phthalocyanine green

lamp black

Above Pigments are obtained from both organic and inorganic substances. Among those shown are a number of inorganic materials – natural earths in the background and minerals in the foreground.

PAINT & COLOUR MIXING

Whether you choose to buy your paints ready mixed or to mix your own, it is essential to understand the composition and uses of different types of paint and how colours are mixed so you can choose with confidence.

Paint

Today's household paints have been improved vastly over the years: pigments are more permanent and the mediums have been modified so the paints are more easily and successfully applied. Previously, paints used either water or oil to carry their pigment, and although linseed oil is still important in the industry, paints are now usually a blend of synthetic resins, oil-based paints generally in the form of oil-modified alkyd resins, and emulsions in the form of PVA and PVC copolymers. However, improving the effectiveness of paint has in many cases also meant using potentially toxic petro-chemicals and other substances that deplete natural, non-replaceable resources and pollute the atmosphere. Further, these paints do not allow the surface they cover to breathe. Today there appears to be a growing awareness of the advantages of certain of the more traditional coverings, such as limewash and soft distemper, coupled with a more responsible view of the effects of some paints on the environment. A number of companies are producing organic pigments, paints, binders and solvents – although general knowledge of their benefits and uses is still limited. It is well worth your time to investigate the make-up of the paints you use and consider their application before you begin.

Types of paint For the decorator there are paints that cover plaster, wood, metal, tiles, concrete and lining paper. There are spray paints, non-drip paints, solid emulsions, and a slow move to more water-based formulations. The range is greater than that offered in the general do-it-yourself store; you may have to buy some at specialist paint shops. However, there are basically two types of paint for decorating: oil-based and water-based. There are also three main categories of finish: flat (matt), mid sheen – which is variously called eggshell, silk, satin or semi-gloss, according to the degree of sheen and the manufacturer – and gloss.

Colour mixing

Today there is a far greater range of colours than ever before in ready-mixed paints. And the advantages of buying paint in a can straight off the shelf are fairly obvious – it is easy and you can usually get the same colour again. It is especially difficult to mix dark colours yourself and so a mistake can be expensive – a good case for buying a ready-mix.

However, choosing a pre-mixed paint colour from the postage-stamp-sized sample you get in a paint shop is extremely difficult and testers are not always available in the complete colour range offered. It may be helpful to know that some colours look different when painted on the wall and dry, so it is a good idea to buy a small can to test. Also, it is not always possible to buy or have mixed the exact colour you want or are looking for. Here, mixing your own colours on site makes sense. Essentially, good colour mixing is a matter of experience and instinct. You will discover that with certain colours – especially the saturated ones – there is only one way to achieve it. But with most colour mixing, colours can be arrived at in various ways. The paint you start with is important. Either a water-based or an oil-based one can be used, but once you start with one medium, you must stick to it. To make a light or mid-tone colour, use white – but not brilliant white – paint as a base. A transparent base (oily, transparent glaze, emulsion glaze or binder) can be used to give deep colours. While a transparent base will look milky when wet in its can, it will dry clear. To get the right proportion of colour, start by mixing a small amount, making careful note of the quantities of each.

Secondary colours Primaries cannot be mixed, and it is difficult to mix good secondary colours on your own: we recommend that you buy them and alter the colours to suit your needs. However, it is helpful to understand the theory so you can achieve the next step – even have a picture of the colour wheel in front of you. In general, if your colours are going muddy, you are either trying to mix colours that are opposite to each other on the wheel, or there are too many different colours in the mix. It will take time and patience experimenting with colours before you will begin to feel confident. If you are trying to create a secondary colour, like violet for example, you may find you get a dull brownish colour, not the good clear one you were looking for. A good rule of thumb in getting a clear mix is to combine the pigments that harmonize, or verge towards each other on the wheel, not away. So for a good violet you should choose colours on the violet-red and violet-blue side, not on the orange-red or green-blue side of the wheel. Greens are also very difficult to mix. To get a good clean one, start with a greenish blue – like Prussian blue – and mix it with a lemon yellow. (A reddish blue and an orange-yellow would give your green a brown tinge.) Tertiary colours are easier to mix because they are even less 'pure'.

To give brilliance and depth to a colour An intense colour cannot be mixed but relies on pure, high-quality pigment, unmuddied, unmuted and without any white. To apply an intense colour, suspend it in a glaze, over a white ground. A bright colour cannot be made brighter, but you can enhance its essential characteristics by adding more pigment. But if you add white paint, the brilliance will be quickly lost and warmer colours will be cooled.

To make an intense colour muted or more subtle Again, suspend your colour in a glaze, then add a little of the complementary of the hue you are using. The colour becomes more subtle, then increasingly muddied; eventually it turns a darkish brown.

To make a colour darker Be careful about adding black to darken a colour; it will be deadened very quickly. As with making a colour muted, once it is suspended in a glaze you can add the complementary of your hue or mix in raw umber. You can also start with a darker base or add more of the original pigment.

Mixing pale colours If you are mixing pale colours, start with a white base, usually in a large tin. Pour off a small amount of white into a second container and add your pigments or colour to it until you get the right mix. The first mix should be the right hue but will probably look somewhat darker in tone than when the larger amount of white is added. You can test the dry colour quickly by using a hair dryer.

Adding colour with stainers or artist's colours Universal stainers come in various makes and are used to create paint colour. Their disadvantage is their limited range. You can, however, extend the range of colours by adding artist's acrylic to white emulsion or adding artist's oil colour to eggshell, satinwood or a gloss paint. With artist's colours as a source, you can achieve a larger and more sophisticated range than you can with stainers, but remember that artist's oils have no driers in them, so the base paint stays oily and the paint takes longer to dry. Also, oils and acrylics are not as concentrated as universal stainers.

Specific colour recipes – showing how colours work together – follow, to give you a visual picture of colour mixing.

Steps in colour mixing
The simplest way to mix a colour is as follows:
1 Take a pot of white paint (gloss, eggshell or emulsion)
2 Add a few drops of universal stainer
3 Stir thoroughly
4 Test the colour
5 Add more stainer if necessary

To mix your own colour from emulsion and artist's acrylics:
1 First mix the acrylic colour with water to dilute it and remove any lumps
2 Pour into the emulsion a little at a time, testing frequently on a previously prepared surface. Stir thoroughly
3 Test the colour
4 Add more colour if necessary

To add artist's oil colour to an oil-based paint:
1 Mix the oil colour with a little white spirit or turpentine to remove any lumps
2 Add it to the paint (eggshell, satinwood or gloss) and stir thoroughly
3 Test the colour, remembering that oils take longer to dry in base paint than stainers or acrylics
4 Add more colour if necessary

Steps in painting
The maximum protection for a surface is achieved by coating it with layers. A basic minimum would comprise a priming coat, an undercoat – to cover the primer and provide a key for subsequent coats – and a finishing or top coat that gives a surface its final appearance and texture.

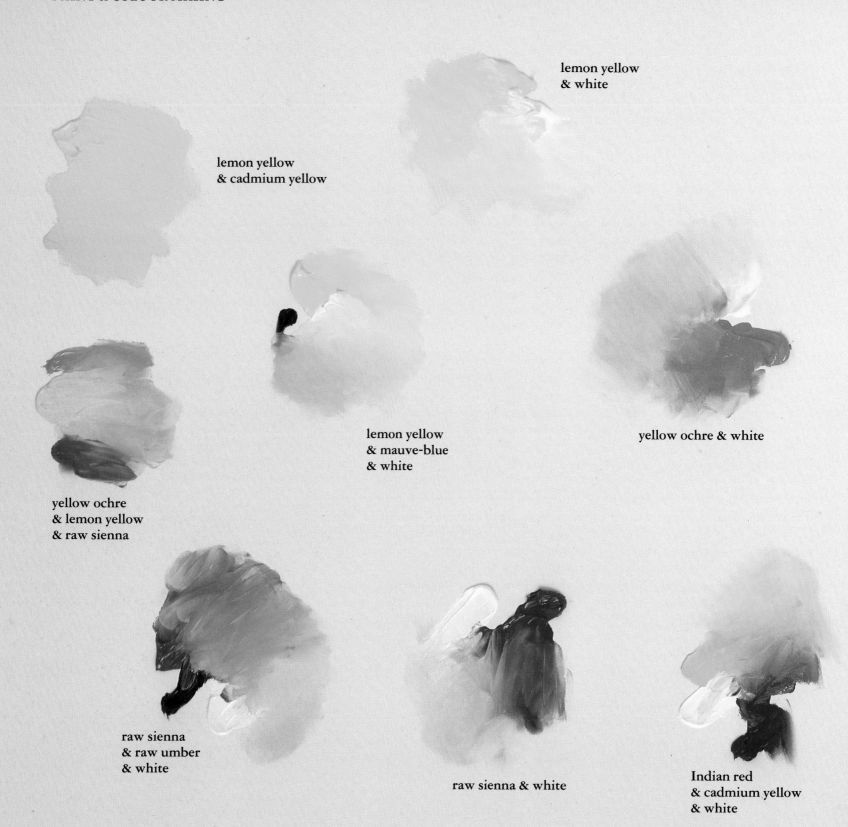

lemon yellow
& white

lemon yellow
& cadmium yellow

lemon yellow
& mauve-blue
& white

yellow ochre & white

yellow ochre
& lemon yellow
& raw sienna

raw sienna
& raw umber
& white

raw sienna & white

Indian red
& cadmium yellow
& white

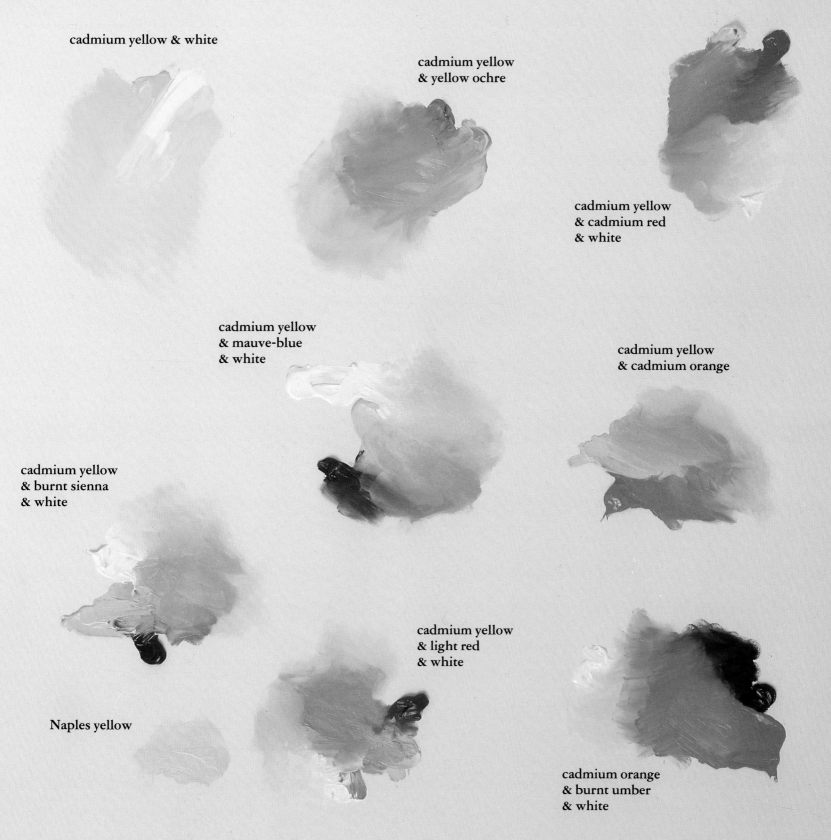

cadmium yellow & white

cadmium yellow
& yellow ochre

cadmium yellow
& cadmium red
& white

cadmium yellow
& mauve-blue
& white

cadmium yellow
& cadmium orange

cadmium yellow
& burnt sienna
& white

cadmium yellow
& light red
& white

Naples yellow

cadmium orange
& burnt umber
& white

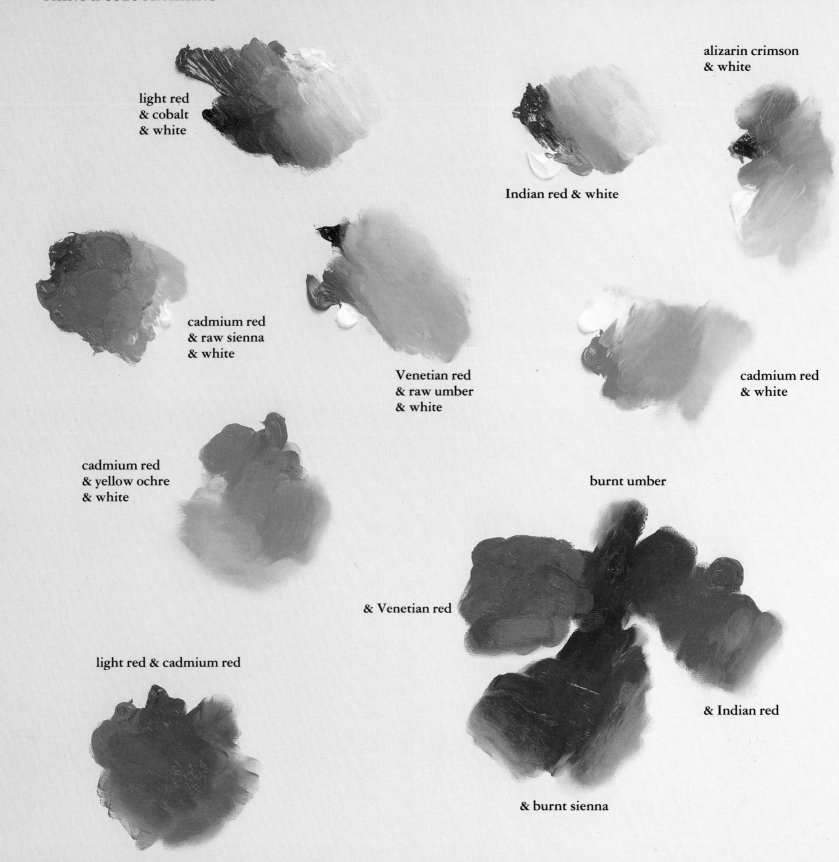

light red
& cobalt
& white

alizarin crimson
& white

Indian red & white

cadmium red
& raw sienna
& white

Venetian red
& raw umber
& white

cadmium red
& white

cadmium red
& yellow ochre
& white

burnt umber

& Venetian red

light red & cadmium red

& Indian red

& burnt sienna

alizarin crimson
& ultramarine

alizarin crimson
& viridian

cobalt violet
& white

alizarin crimson
& burnt umber

alizarin crimson
& burnt sienna

mauve-blue & white

cadmium red
& ultramarine

magenta & white

permanent rose
& white

Brown or yellow pigments may be added
to purples to give muted colours

cobalt & Prussian blue

cobalt & cerulean blue
& white

cobalt & cadmium orange & white

ultramarine
& alizarin crimson
& white

ultramarine
& mauve-blue
& white

ultramarine
& cadmium orange
& white

cobalt
& ultramarine

cobalt & white

ultramarine & white

cobalt
& ultramarine
& white

Prussian blue
& raw umber
& white

cobalt & burnt umber & white

ultramarine
& raw umber
& white

cerulean blue
& viridian
& white

ultramarine
& burnt umber
& white

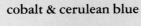

cobalt & cerulean blue

cerulean blue
& raw umber
& white

cobalt
& cerulean blue
& raw umber
& white

viridian
& cerulean blue
& white

viridian
& cobalt

viridian & raw umber

viridian
& raw umber
& white

Prussian blue
& lemon yellow

oxide of chromium & white

oxide of chromium
& yellow ochre
& white

terre verte & white

cerulean blue & viridian

lemon yellow
& viridian

lemon yellow
& black

cadmium yellow
& black

yellow ochre
& Prussian blue
& white

lemon yellow
& cerulean blue

cadmium yellow
& ultramarine
& white

lemon yellow
& cobalt
& white

lemon yellow
& cobalt

lemon yellow
& viridian
& white

burnt umber
& alizarin crimson

burnt umber
& burnt sienna

burnt sienna
& yellow ochre

burnt umber
& cadmium red

raw umber
& white

burnt umber & white

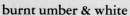

raw sienna
& raw umber
& white

yellow ochre
& cadmium yellow
& white

yellow ochre
& raw umber
& white

raw sienna
& white

Naples yellow
& white

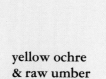

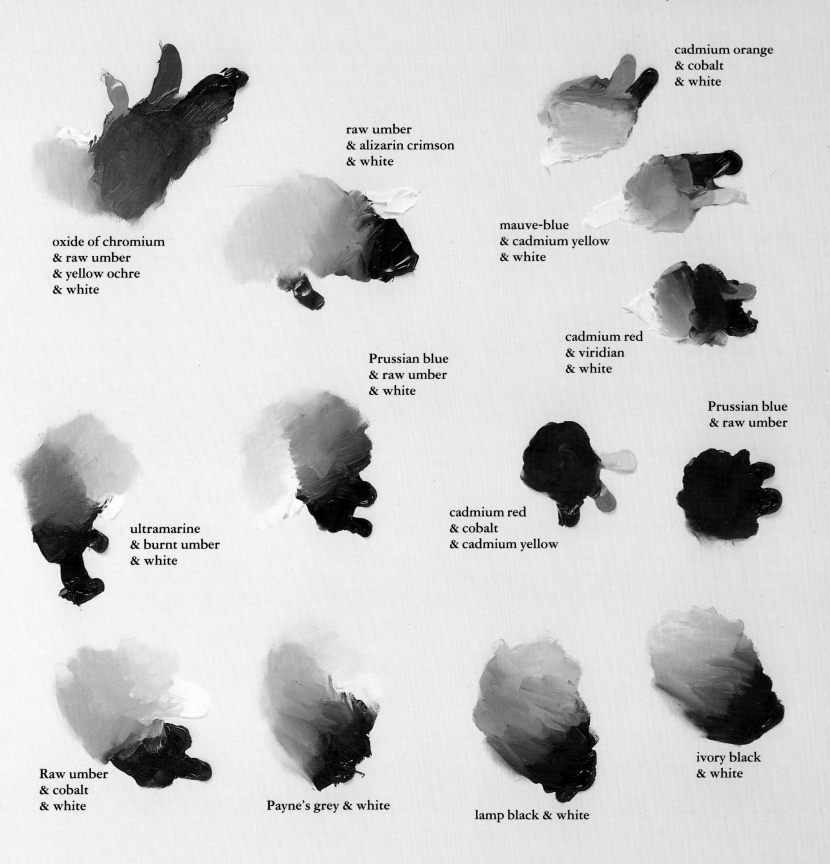

cadmium orange
& cobalt
& white

raw umber
& alizarin crimson
& white

oxide of chromium
& raw umber
& yellow ochre
& white

mauve-blue
& cadmium yellow
& white

cadmium red
& viridian
& white

Prussian blue
& raw umber
& white

Prussian blue
& raw umber

ultramarine
& burnt umber
& white

cadmium red
& cobalt
& cadmium yellow

Raw umber
& cobalt
& white

Payne's grey & white

lamp black & white

ivory black
& white

185

MATERIALS
Oil-based paint

Oil-based paints are more slow drying than water-based paints. Their great advantage is that they are reasonably tough and generally washable; a disadvantage is having to wash out brushes and equipment in solvents, not water, and having to create a 'key' on the surface to be painted. The traditional form of oil paint was a mix of white lead, raw linseed oil, a solvent in the form of turpentine, driers and pigment. With recent advances in technology, linseed oil has been replaced by combinations of oils and resins that are more stable, that flow more readily and give a higher gloss. Oil-based paints come in different finishes.

Flat finish (matt) This looks like emulsion paint but it is oil-based. It is comparatively difficult to find except through specialist paint suppliers, but it is fairly easy to apply and has a satisfying look and feel to it. Although oil-based, it is not a very durable finish and is not recommended in areas of heavy traffic. However, although once almost obsolete, there is a growing demand for it which is being catered for by a few of the bigger paint manufacturers. A flat finish can also be achieved by adding matting agent (a compound that decreases gloss) to an oil-based eggshell, giving a wide range of colour possibilities.

Mid-sheen finish This is also known as 'eggshell' paint to convey that it dries to the sort of sheen found on the shell of an egg. It is washable, easy to apply and comes in a wide range of colours. Although it is usually not found under this name in the average do-it-yourself shop, a good paint shop should have it. It is sometimes referred to as semi-gloss or satinwood, however these have a higher sheen than a true eggshell – which usually lies halfway between a matt and a gloss. It is a very good base for such decorative paint techniques as stippling, ragging and so on and can be used on walls as well as on woodwork.

Gloss finish This is a very shiny paint finish that is generally used on woodwork rather than on walls. Although it is washable and

tough, if chipped, the flaws are noticeable. It also shows up imperfections in the surface more than a mid-sheen would.

Water-based paint

Water-based paints (also known as emulsion paints) are easier to apply than oils, although they are not so tough and hardwearing. Emulsion consists of two liquids: the first is a polymer; the second is usually water. Cheap emulsions have poor covering power and are generally not worth buying. Emulsions are wipeable but not washable. Emulsion finishes are categorized in the same way as oil-based finishes.

Flat finish Flat emulsion and matt vinyl paints have more sheen than flat oil-based paints for walls and ceilings and they are inexpensive, quick to apply and fast drying. They can also be used as a base for some decorative finishes and some types can be applied in a single coat.

Mid-sheen finish There are a number of mid-sheen emulsions on the market, usually called vinyl silk, sometimes satin. They have a slight sheen and are generally used on walls rather than woodwork. The coverage is not as good as that of flat finishes, but they will withstand more cleaning. In the last year or two an acrylic quick-drying eggshell has come on to the market for use on wood.

Gloss finish There are no truly high-gloss water-based paints. There have been attempts to introduce them over the years, but either the house painter's natural conservatism or the fact that they have not been as durable as oil-based glosses has led to them being withdrawn. However, with recent advances in acrylics, semi-gloss paints have become available, and a high-gloss may be on general sale in the fairly near future. PVA adhesive (a water-based glue that can be thinned and dries clear and shiny like varnish) can be brushed over emulsion to give it a higher sheen. Not as easy to find is a gloss emulsion glaze that will do much the same.

Varnish

Varnish is a transparent coating for surfaces.

Like paint, it can be oil- or water-based and is also available in matt, eggshell and gloss finishes. Oil-based varnish is manufactured from oils, resins and a solvent, while the water-based is usually based on acrylic resins. Usually varnish is used to protect a surface, giving a lustrous finish that brings out the colour underneath and adds a look of gloss. Less strong, but more often used perhaps in decorative painting, are the matt and eggshell finishes. In order to provide maximum durability and clarity with a low sheen, the initial coats of a multi-layer process should always be in gloss. Oil-based varnishes have a tendency to yellow, and care must be taken in their selection. Yacht varnishes, for example, are formulated to provide protection against the harsh conditions of the sea, the corrosive effect of sea-water and UV rays from the sun. While excellent over ships' timbers, their inherent yellowness may make your pale blue stippled wall appear green. The emulsion glaze already mentioned is sometimes referred to as varnish, albeit a very weak one. It is used as a coating for non-washable wallpaper in order to make it spongeable, but it can also be used to give limited protection to other surfaces. True water-based varnishes have begun to appear in the last few years, some sufficiently durable to be used on floors. They are good for light-coloured surfaces because they do not yellow, and they are very quick drying. Varnish can have pigment added to it to 'float' a colour over a surface. Although sometimes confused with a glaze, it has very different properties.

COLOURING MATTER
Powder pigments

These can be found in specialist shops and they can be added to any medium, both oil- and water-based. They are usually mixed in a base before they are used. They are classified according to their origin. The inorganic are the native earths, such as the ochres and umbers. These also include the artificially prepared mineral colours such as cadmium red and zinc white. The organic are the animal and vegetable colours such as indigo, madder, cochineal and Indian yellow. The synthetic organic pigments include alizarin crimson and mauve.

Universal stainers

These provide colour in a vehicle that is soluble in both water- and oil-based paints and they can be found in most decorating and do-it-yourself shops.

Artist's oil paints

Oil colours come in two ranges: artist's and student's. The first is more expensive and contains the highest grade of materials. Both the resistance to fading and the tinting power of these paints are greater than in the student's ranges, which are much cheaper. It is worth experimenting with the different ranges and also the makes, as you will often find that you prefer one manufacturer's version of a colour to another's. Unlike universal stainers, they can only be used with oil-based paints. They can also be added to glazes and oil-based varnishes.

Artist's acrylics

These are pigments mixed in an acrylic medium. They are thinned with water, but they dry quickly to form a tough, flexible, waterproof film. To avoid ruining your brushes rest them in a jar of water while painting to keep them from drying out. Use a piece of plate glass as a palette, as it can be scraped clean with a razor blade. They are especially good for stencilling because they dry quickly and can be used for colouring other water-based paints.

SPECIAL PAINTS & FINISHES

In addition to the usual decorating paints and finishes in oil- or water-based paints, there are a number of others that deserve mention. These include limewash, distemper and glazes.

Distemper

Distemper is basically whiting, or ground chalk, bound with either glue size, casein or an 'emulsion' of oil and water. There are two types, both of which possess characteristic mattness and a slightly chalky surface.

Soft distemper This is the size-bound type, called 'soft' because the dried coating remains soluble in water and is easily removed by washing. Until about twenty years ago it was the standard finish for ceilings where its powdery quality was not considered a serious drawback. It can be applied to walls but cannot be cleaned, and the dustiness may be a nuisance if accidentally brushed against. Experience of trying to remove multiple layers of emulsion paints from elaborate cornices and plasterwork to restore their definition has led to new interest in it.

All the ingredients to make distemper should be available from a specialist decorator's shop, although a prepared paste designed for use on ceilings is still being manufactured if you wish to avoid the trouble. Recently a couple of firms dealing with traditional paints have introduced soft distemper in 'kit' form.

Recipe for soft distemper

Place 1.4 kgs (3 lbs) of whiting in a bucket and cover with fresh water. Leave overnight to soak. Pour off the excess water, and add one-half litre (1 pint) of hot size prepared by dissolving 30 grams (1 ounce) of animal glue size in a pint of hot water. Stir thoroughly and allow to stand until cold. It should resemble a thin jelly, which when worked up will have excellent covering powers. (If you see lumps or skin on the mixture before using, strain it carefully through muslin or a fine sieve.) It will dry to an off-white colour unless you add a small quantity of blue to brighten the white. You can colour it with other pigments, of course, but these should be added before the size. When dry, the distemper will appear much lighter than in its wet state. (Very porous surfaces should be primed with a thin coat of size before the distemper is applied.)

Washable distemper As the name implies, washable distempers are capable of being cleaned to varying degrees. Also known as water paints, they are still produced by a number of small manufacturers. There are two main types: those bound with an emulsion of oil in water – or varnish – and those bound with casein. Being more durable than soft distemper they are suitable for walls. They also have the advantage of not needing to be removed before redecorating. The recipes for this sort of distemper are rather more complex and it is best bought ready-made.

Limewash

Until recently limewash was the traditional coating for the outside of buildings and in certain places it is still used. It gives a soft matt finish that should last for a couple of years before needing another coat. The characteristic weathering is part of its appeal and the earth colours that are traditionally mixed with it add greatly to the attraction. Limewash has very important practical advantages in that it allows the surface it covers to breathe. This is of particular significance in houses built before the mid nineteenth century which might not have had a damp course. The ingredients for limewash are very simple and can be found at a few specialized outlets, but great care must be taken in making it, as it is extremely caustic in its wet state. If you intend to make your own, it is safest to use lime putty rather than quicklime. Ensure that you are wearing protective goggles, gloves and overalls before beginning work.

Recipe for limewash

Place a litre of lime putty (about 3 trowelfuls) in a 10-litre (5-gallon) bucket with a cupful of skimmed milk. Stir well until it becomes a smooth paste. Add more skimmed milk until the mixture has the consistency of thin cream. If pigment is to be added, it should be mixed in a jar with a little hot water and stirred well beforehand. Add the pigment to the creamy mix and stir well, then sieve into a second bucket. Rinse the first bucket and remove any grit. At this stage check the colour by brushing some out on a piece of white paper and drying. Adjust if necessary. Dilute the mixture further until it has the consistency of milk, then sieve again into the first bucket. It may now be applied.

It is important to observe the following

points in order to get successful results. The surface must be brushed and well dampened down first. A garden spray is ideal for keeping the area to be painted wet. Do not apply when the sun is particularly strong, and do not try to accelerate the drying. Several thin coats are better than one or two thick ones. Lime will destroy certain pigments. Generally the earth colours are safe, but check first with your supplier.

There are several methods for making durable limewash for outside use. The one we have given here is both easy to make and is thought to have the least harmful effect on porous masonry. As the use of limewash invariably means re-treatment with the same – it must be removed or covered with an alkaline primer – it is important to consider the implications before using it indoors. Unless you feel fully confident about using this medium, we recommend you have it painted for you.

Casein

Made from skimmed milk, casein is often used as a binder in both limewash and distemper. A reaction with an alkaline substance will produce a very powerful adhesive. It is also used as a paint, with lime or another substance added to break down its inherent stickiness. It gives a natural finish. In its purest form it is available as a powder which must be used fresh for best results.

Recipe for casein paint

Take 60 grams (2 ounces) of powdered casein and sift slowly into one-third litre (half-pint) of water, stirring slowly to avoid lumps. When smooth, add 30 grams (1 ounce) of ammonium carbonate and stir. Allow the mixture to stand for about 30 minutes before stirring in another one-third litre (half-pint) of water. Into this you can add pigments that have been ground carefully in water. This will produce a quick-drying matt finish that is very tough and water-resistant. Keep brushes in water when they are not being used and clean them carefully afterwards.

Limed oak finish

Real limed oak is oak with lime putty rubbed in. This finish gives a similar look; it is a treatment that whitens wood but allows the grain to show through. It is suitable only on woods with a strong grain, such as oak or pitch pine.

Recipe for limed oak finish

Take a strong decorator's wire brush and brush firmly in the direction of the wood grain to remove any soft wood. Wipe off any resulting dust. Then take a soft cloth and dip it into an eggshell paint tinted with light colour (off-white, pale blue and pale green are effective). Rub the paint over the wood, making certain that the paint fills the gaps left by wire brushing. Then take a clean cloth slightly dampened with white spirit, and wipe off the excess paint so colour is left only in the gaps. Allow to dry. A coat of liming wax can be added to protect the wood. It can also be used on its own for a more subtle effect than with paint.

Glaze

Glaze is a transparent, oily medium to which pigment is added and then it is painted over a base allowing the base colour to show through – particularly when it is broken up with a rag or brush. A glaze can also be used simply over a colour to change its look. It is sometimes called scumble glaze. It has more body than a varnish and is not totally transparent. It is designed to retain the impression of the brush, comb or rag used to 'figure' it.

Most of the broken colour finishes, such as ragging, dragging and stippling, can be achieved with the following recipe. However, there are many different recipes for glaze, and you must be prepared to adjust the mix to suit the particular task in hand.

Recipe for glaze

Make a mixture of 50 per cent transparent oil glaze (often known as scumble glaze) and 50 per cent white spirit. As a rule of thumb, half a litre (1 pint) of this mix, with the relevant pigments, will be sufficient to cover a room of 4 metres by 4 metres (13 feet by 13 feet). As well as using artist's oils you can also use universal stainers or oil-based paint to provide the colouring matter. If you want pale tints, it is often best to sacrifice a bit of translucency by adding the colour in the form of a ready-mixed oil-based paint. You will need to experiment with the proportion of colour to glaze: start by making a small quantity, and if it is not right, it can be wiped off. You can achieve a number of effects by spreading glaze thinly or thickly and by varying the amount of colour. Getting the knack is a process of trial and error. If ragging, for example, paint the glaze on in manageable areas, say 1 metre by 1 metre (approximately 3 feet by 3 feet), being careful to spread the glaze on thinly and evenly, especially at the edges. Then rag off the glaze by dabbing it firmly with a clean bunched cotton cloth, replacing the cloth as soon as it is wet. Work this way section by section until you have completed the room. For extra protection, you can varnish over when dry.

Lacquer walls

Lacquers used to be based on special oriental tree resin. The material was poisonous and the work time-consuming, so lacquering was suitable only for small objects or furniture. Today whole walls are painted to mimic this look – particularly popular are deep crimson reds and greens that are given a gloss finish with varnish. There are a number of methods of lacquering – one quick way is with a base of gloss paint covered with varnish. A richer, deeper effect can be achieved by painting on a bright, oil-based colour over which a deeper scumble glaze of the same colour can be applied. Any excess is taken off, then the remaining glaze blended in with a badger-hair brush so it looks polished. Leave to dry. When dry, add a layer of varnish with a gloss or mid-sheen finish.

BIBLIOGRAPHY

Ayres, James *The Shell Book of the Home in Britain* Faber & Faber, London and Boston, 1981

Battersby, Martin *The Decorative Thirties* Studio Vista, London, 1971; reprinted Herbert Press, London and Watson-Guptill Publications, New York, 1988

Battersby, Martin *The Decorative Twenties* Studio Vista, London, 1969; reprinted Herbert Press, London and Watson-Guptill Publications, New York, 1988

Gaunt, William and M.D.E. Clayton-Stamm *William De Morgan* Studio Vista, London, 1971, and NYGS, New York, 1971

Goethe, Johann Wolfgang von *Theory of Colours* Frank Cass, London, 1967 and The MIT Press, London and Cambridge, Massachusetts, 1970

Harley, R. D. *Artists' Pigments C. 1600–1835* Butterworth Scientific, London and Butterworth Publishers, Stoneham, Massachusetts, 1982

Hicks, David *Style and Design* Viking Penguin, Harmondsworth and New York, 1987

Innes, Jocasta *Paint Magic* Frances Lincoln, London and Pantheon Books, New York, 1987

Ionides, Basil *Colour and Interior Decoration* Country Life Ltd, London, 1926

Itten, Johannes *Art of Colour* Van Nostrand Reinhold, London, 1961 and New York, 1974

Kornerup, A. and Wanscher, J. H. *Methuen Handbook of Colour* Methuen, London, 1989 and Heinemann Ed. Books Inc, New Hampshire, 1978

Mayer, Ralph *The Artist's Handbook of Materials and Techniques* Faber and Faber, London, 1987 and Viking, New York, 1981

Miller, Judith and Martin *Period Style* Mitchell Beazley, London 1989; as *Period Design and Furnishing* Random House, New York, 1989

Rossotti, Hazel *Colour* Penguin, London, 1983; as *Colour: Why The World Isn't Grey* Princeton University Press, New Jersey, 1985

Thornton, Peter *Authentic Decor: The Domestic Interior 1620–1920* Weidenfeld & Nicolson, London, 1985 and Viking, New York, 1984

Varley, Helen (ed.) *Colour* Mitchell Beazley, London, 1980

Walch, Margaret *The Colour Source Book* Thames and Hudson, London, 1979

Wilcox, Michael *Blue and Yellow Don't Make Green* Collins, London, 1989

Zelanski, Paul and Fisher, Mary Pat *Colour: For Designers and Artists* The Herbert Press, 1989; as *Color* Prentice Hall Editions, New York, 1989

USEFUL ADDRESSES

GLAZE SUPPLIERS

J. W. Bollom & Co. Ltd
J. T. Keep
15 Theobald's Road
London WC1X 8SN
071 242 0313

40 Port Street
Manchester M1 2EQ
061 236 7715

Unit 2, Birmingham Road
Allesley
Nr. Coventry CV5 9QE
0203 405151

121 South Liberty Lane
Ashton Vale
Bristol BS3 2SZ
0272 665151

Craig & Rose PLC
677/693 Princes Road
Dartford DA2 6EE
0322 222481

172 Leith Walk
Edinburgh EH6 5EB
031 554 1131

30 Lawmoor Road
Glasgow G5 0UX
041 429 4347

Fiddes & Son Ltd
Florence Works, Brindley Road
Cardiff CF1 7TX
0222 340323
(mail order and nationwide delivery service)

J. H. Ratcliffe & Co. (Paints) Ltd
135A Linaker Street
Southport PR8 5DF
0704 37999
(glazes, scumbles and specialist brushes)

POWDER PIGMENTS

Brodie & Middleton Ltd
68 Drury Lane
London WC2B 5SP
071 836 3289
(also gold leaf, specialist brushes)

L. Cornelissen & Son Ltd
105 Great Russell Street
London WC1B 3RY
071 636 1045
(also gilding materials, specialist brushes)

E. Ploton Ltd
273 Archway Road
London N6 5AA
081 348 0315
(also glazes, specialist brushes and mail order service)

SPECIALIST DECORATOR'S MATERIALS

C. Brewer & Sons Ltd
327 Putney Bridge Road
London SW15 2PG
081 788 9335
(glazes, specialist brushes)

Paint Service Co. (Victoria) Ltd
19 Eccleston Street
London SW1W 9LX
071 730 6408
071 730 7458
(glazes, stainers, varnishes, specialist brushes)

Whistler Brush Co.
128 Fortune Green Road
London NW6
071 794 3130
(specialist brushes)

SPECIALIST PAINTS

Auro Organic Paints (GB) Ltd
White Horse House
Ashdon
Nr. Saffron Walden
Essex CB10 2ET
0799 84888
(casein paint, plant, earth and mineral pigments)

H. J. Chard & Sons
Feeder Road
Bristol BS2 0TJ
0272 777681
(materials for limewashing and nationwide delivery service)

John Oliver Ltd
33 Pembridge Road
London W11 3HG
071 221 6466

Papers and Paints Ltd
4 Park Walk
London SW10 0AD
071 352 8626
(also specialist decorator's materials)

The Society for the Protection of Ancient Buildings
37 Spital Square
London E1 6DY
071 377 1644
(technical advice on the use of paints and limewash)

INDEX